around LONDON with KIDS

by Alex Wijeratna

CREDITS
Writer: Alex Wijeratna

Editors: Jacinta O'Halloran, Maria Teresa Hart
Editorial Production: Carolyn Roth
Production/Manufacturing: Angela L. McLean

Design: Fabrizio La Rocca, *creative director*;
Tigist Getachew, *designer*
Cover Art and Design: Jessie Hartland
Flip Art and Illustration: Rico Lins, Keren Ora Admoni/
Rico Lins Studio

ABOUT THE WRITER
While bringing up his two daughters in London, Alex Wijeratna is a long-standing restaurant reviewer for Fodor's London, and has written on the arts to architecture for *The Times* of London, *Guardian*, *Daily Mail*, and *Independent*.

Fodor's Around London with Kids

Copyright © 2013 by Fodor's Travel, a division of Random House, Inc.

Fodor's is a registered trademark of Random House, Inc. All rights reserved. Published in the United States by Fodor's Travel, a division of Random House, Inc., New York, and simultaneously in Canada by Random House of Canada Limited, Toronto. Distributed by Random House, Inc., New York.

ISBN: 978-1-4000-0744-8
ISSN: 1533-5321
Fourth Edition

Important Tip
Although all prices, opening times, and other details in this book are based on information supplied to us at press time, changes occur all the time in the travel world, and Fodor's cannot accept responsibility for facts that become outdated or for inadvertent errors or omissions. So always confirm information when it matters, especially if you're making a detour to visit a specific place.

Special Sales
This book is available for special discounts for bulk purchases for sales promotions or premiums. Special editions, including personalized covers, excerpts of existing books, and corporate imprints, can be created in large quantities for special needs. For more information, write to Special Markets/Premium Sales, 1745 Broadway, MD 3-1, New York, NY 10019, or e-mail specialmarkets@randomhouse.com.

PRINTED IN THE UNITED STATES OF AMERICA
10 9 8 7 6 5 4 3 2

MANY THANKS!

More than once I thought my two young kids would mutiny as I dragged them off for yet another jam-packed agenda of brilliant London palaces, Royal parks, quirky museums, and *gran turismo* attractions in pursuit of the quintessential review. They didn't—mutiny, that is—and had a blast, and so did their parents, who got to see many long-lost, lesser known, and new sights from a child's perspective. So thank you, girls, for your stamina and enthusiasm during my persnickety gumshoe investigations. My eldest was convinced I would morph into a *National Geographic* reporter as I picked up the scent of a new find, and my youngest was pleasantly surprised when she discovered that she had, after all, enjoyed herself visiting a "boys' " museum—like HMS *Belfast,* or the Imperial War Museum.

We enjoyed attentive treatment from many attractions' education and information experts, whose detailed advice was a boon—in particular, the staff of the National Gallery, Museum of London, British Museum, Tate Britain, the Courtauld Gallery, and Westminster Abbey. You provided an invaluable inside track. The press teams who ensured that info was in the right place at the right time are too numerous to mention, as are the friends, relatives, and their kids who reported faithfully on their recent missions and came back for more. What a team! I'm sure the fruits of your labors will make other visitors' experiences to London—the unofficial *greatest* kids' city in the world!—all the more enjoyable.

—Alex Wijeratna

GOOD TIMES GALORE

WIGGLE & GIGGLE Give your kids a chance to stick out their tongues at you. Start by making a face, then have the next person imitate you and add a gesture of his own—snapping fingers, winking, clapping, sneezing, or the like. The next person mimics the first two and adds a third gesture, and so on.

JUNIOR OPERA During a designated period of time, have your kids sing everything they want to say.

THE QUIET GAME Need a good giggle—or a moment of calm to figure out your route? The driver sets a time limit and everybody must be silent. The last person to make a sound wins.

FUN TIMES A TO Z

GET READY, GET SET!

Packed with world-class museums, historic buildings, royal palaces, gory castles, and more than a thousand years of culture, London has enormous appeal for every kid, from tots to teenagers. Over the last few years (thanks, in part, to preparations for the 2012 Olympic Games and Royal Jubilee), just about every tourist institution in the city has had a major face-lift, with updated displays and more button-pushing computer games, apps, fiber-optic displays, and devices that help kids find out more about what they're seeing. Outside, walks by the Thames or cruises on the river reveal London both old and ultranew. A ride in an open-top bus gives a sense of the location of the city's neighborhoods and landmarks, or you can simply stroll from royal park to royal park to escape the noise and bustle. That's London on the cheap, and if the weather's sunny, at its best.

If you're planning a trip to London, the options can be overwhelming. That's where this book comes in, with 68 ways to have a terrific couple of hours or an entire day, from historic sights to the hands-on, whiz-bang activities of the Science Museum. To ensure that kids don't get culture-dazed, break up a museum day with a pedalo or picnic in a nearby park or some other outdoor activity. Use the neighborhood directory (All Around Town) and the thematic directory (Something for Everyone) at the back of the book to help you make your plans.

SAVING MONEY
Most national museums and galleries, such as the National Gallery, Science Museum, Natural History Museum, and National Maritime Museum, have free entry. You'll pay only for special exhibitions. Some attractions offer free admission one day a week or after a certain time in the afternoon (usually an hour or two before closing). Still, London's independent attractions will dig into your wallet big-time. We list only

regular adult, student (with ID), and kids' prices, in pounds sterling; children under the ages specified are free.

Ask at the ticket booth whether any discounts are offered for a particular status or affiliation (but don't forget to bring your ID). Discounts are often available for senior citizens. Many attractions offer family tickets (usually two adults and two children) or annual or long-term memberships. Prices vary, but the memberships often pay for themselves if you visit several times. Sometimes there are other perks: newsletters or magazines, previews, and shop discounts.

Look for coupons, which might save you money or provide a child's free admission, and check the attraction's own website; more often than not, it will save you money to buy tickets in advance online. Hotel desks often carry Theatre Pair coupons, which allow you to buy two tickets at half price for selected theaters. The TKTS booth, open daily (though Sunday hours are 10:30 to 4:30) in Leicester Square, sells selected West End theater tickets at up to half price for same-day performances. Some groups of attractions (such as Madame Tussauds and Historic Royal Palaces) offer good-value combination passes. If you're traveling around Britain, look into VisitBritain's Great Britain Heritage Pass and English Heritage's Overseas Visitor pass.

Consider money-saving tickets for the tube and bus. Oyster cards, sold at tube ticket booths, are a good deal. Kids under 16 travel free on buses and Tube trains. Excellent-value Visitor Travelcards, sold only in the United States, can be purchased from BritRail or Rail Europe. Some London passes cover not only attractions but transport as well. The London Pass includes around 55 top attractions, boat and bus trips, and restaurant discounts. It comes in one- to six-day versions and starts at £46 for adults. You can buy the London Pass on the Web (londonpass.com), by phone (tel. 0870/242–9988) before you arrive, or from Tourist Information Centres (at Heathrow Airport and Victoria and Liverpool Street stations) and at London Transport Travel Information Centres. The Historic Royal Palaces pass is £83 for a family up to six kids, which offers annual unlimited access to the Tower of London, Hampton Court Palace, and other attractions.

EATING OUT

To save money and still dine well, try lunch deals, or check out London's many ethnic restaurants. Chinatown is colorful, and the city has many Indian and casual Italian restaurants. Gastro-pubs are more budget-wise than fancy restaurants, and generally more family-friendly, too. Those in this guide have been confirmed for family-friendliness, and www.pubs.com has more information. Among the more appealing chains for a quick refueling are Pizza Express, Giraffe, Ed's Easy Diner (hamburgers and fries), Pret a Manger (sandwiches and salads), Wagamama (Japanese noodles), and Strada (pizzas). Picnicking in parks is easy; major supermarkets in central locations carry tasty supplies.

GETTING AROUND

London used to comprise distinct villages, and neighborhoods still retain their individuality. There are 32 different boroughs (administrative districts), and the name of the borough is often given on street signs. Postal (Zip) codes are loosely geographical, radiating from the center (around Marble Arch) and the City financial district. For example, W1 is west of Marble Arch. Bloomsbury, west of the City, is WC1, while the City itself is EC1. Southwark, just south of the

Thames, is SE1; Buckingham Palace, north of the river but south of W1, is SW1. Confused? Just pick up a tourist map from a visitor center, buy a *Streetfinder* or *London A–Z* from a newsstand, and get a free Tube and bus map from any Underground station, and you'll be fine.

The Underground, or Tube, is the most efficient way of getting around; in-station maps show the train lines. Children under 16 travel free. Buses are cheaper than the Tube but can take longer, although kids will enjoy seeing the sights. Buying individual tickets is the most expensive way of getting around. Buy a One-Day Bus Pass for several bus journeys in one day or an Oyster card if you wish to use the Tube as well. Strollers must be folded on buses and trains during peak hours.

WHEN TO GO

With the exception of seasonal attractions, kid-oriented destinations are naturally busiest when children are out of school—especially weekends, holidays, and summers. Attractions that draw school trips can be swamped with kids, but school groups leave by early afternoon, so weekdays after 2 during the school year can be an excellent time to visit museums, zoos, and aquariums. London's attractions can be particularly crowded during half-term school vacations (generally the third week of October, last week of December, first week of January, third week of February, last week of March, and first week of June). Outdoor attractions may be less crowded after rain.

The hours listed are the basic hours, not necessarily those applicable on public, or "bank" holidays. Some attractions close when schools close, but others add extra hours. Surf the Web; some places may have cool special events if they're open on holidays.

LEARNING ENGLISH

You'll get into the British swing of things in no time. Popular kids' food choices include bangers and mash (sausage and mashed potatoes), fish-and-chips (fried fish and french fries), and, to be extra confusing, crisps (potato chips). "Brilliant" is an oft-heard word for "wonderful," and "trainers" are "sneakers." Referring to transportation, "single" means "one-way," and "return" means "round-trip." Make a detective game of it with your kids, and have fun figuring out the meanings of all the phrases you hear. Brilliant!

RESOURCES AND INFORMATION

The London Tourist Information Centre at Victoria Station (opposite platform 8), and the Britain and London Visitor Centre (1 Regent St.), near Piccadilly Circus, are good resources, with leaflets from independent operators. Check out VisitLondon's website visitlondon. com, for information, deals, and news on kid-friendly attractions. London's free weekly *Time Out* magazine and website timeout.com/london/kids has special sections for kids and families.

FINAL THOUGHTS

Lots of moms, dads, and kids were interviewed to create these suggestions, and we'd love to add yours. Email us your kid-friendly additions at editors@fodors. com (specify the name of the book on the subject line), or write to us at Fodor's Around London with Kids, 1745 Broadway, 5th floor, New York, NY 10019. In the meantime, have fun!

—Alex Wijeratna

BEST BETS

FODOR'S CHOICE
Hampton Court Palace, 48
London Eye, 37
Shakespeare's Globe, 13
Tower of London, 6
Warner Bros. Studio Tour:
The Making of Harry Potter, 4
Westminster Abbey, 2

BEST OUTDOORS
Fat Tire's Royal London Bike Tour, 53
Kensington Gardens, 43
Legoland, 40
Royal Botanic Gardens, Kew, 19
Thames River Cruise, 7

BEST CULTURAL ACTIVITY
Tate Modern, 8

BEST MUSEUM
Museum of London, 31

WACKIEST
London Dungeon, 38

NEW & NOTEWORTHY
Buckingham Palace, 64
Kensington Gardens, 43
London Wetland Centre, 35
Museum of London, 31
Warner Bros. Studio Tour:
The Making of Harry Potter, 4

SOMETHING FOR EVERYONE

A LITTLE KNOWLEDGE
British Library, **66**
Churchill War Rooms, **60**
Covent Garden, **56**
Hunterian Museum, **46**
London Transport Museum, **36**
National Theatre, **25**
Royal Air Force Museum, **20**
Royal Opera House, **15**
Shakespeare's Globe, **13**
South Bank, **11**
Westminster Abbey, **2**

ART ATTACK
Courtauld Gallery, **57**
Kenwood House, **42**
National Gallery, **28**
National Portrait Gallery, **26**
Somerset House, **12**
Tate Britain, **9**
Tate Modern, **8**

COOL 'HOODS
Borough Market, **67**
Chinatown, **61**
Columbia Road Flower Market, **59**
Covent Garden, **56**
West End Show, **3**

CULTURE CLUB
British Library, **66**
British Museum, **65**
Museum of London, **31**
Shakespeare's Globe, **13**
Tate Britain, **9**
Westminster Abbey, **2**

FARMS AND ANIMALS
Battersea Park, **68**
Coram's Fields, **58**
London Wetland Centre, **35**
London Zoo, **34**

TIRE THEM OUT

WATER, WATER EVERYWHERE

WAY UP HIGH

ALL AROUND TOWN

BATTERSEA PARK

Battersea Park is South London's finest park, an inner-city secret gem, and—remarkably—London's only major city-center Thames-side promenade. With riverside walks, several beautiful gardens, playing fields, playgrounds, a contemporary art gallery and regular art fairs, sculpture, a lake with boat rental, a charming little zoo, and more, there is much to see and do here and plenty of energy outlets and appeal for kids.

Opened in 1858, Battersea Park was popular with Victorian Londoners who flocked to its romantic gardens, lake, and waterfalls as a place to relax away from the overcrowded city. Today, the 200-acre park just over from Chelsea Embankment and directly linked by Albert and Chelsea Bridges, is justly popular with locals who still come to bask in its calm oasis. (Yet it is, somehow, off-the-beaten tourist track . . . so shhh!)

Kids can let off steam along the winding paths and open fields and later burrow through tunnels on their tummies and pop up and meet meerkats or spot ring-tail lemurs, otters, coatis, chinchillas, or capuchin monkeys at the Battersea Park Children's Zoo (tel. 020/7924–5826). From giant rabbits to miniature Shetland ponies, monkey mayhem, to a duck

EATS FOR KIDS The **Lemon Tree Café** inside Battersea Park Children's Zoo has snacks and sandwiches. The family-run **La Gondola al Parco** (Rosary Gate, tel. 020/7978–1655) has more filling Italian staples and favorites, plus kids menus. Scoot back over the Thames to the King's Road for soup and Belgium tartines at shared wooden tables at **Le Pain Quotidien** (201 King's Rd., tel. 020/3657–6941). Farther along the King's Rd., you'll find £7.50 kids menus like roast chicken with new potatoes and salad at the smart **Gallery Mess** (Duke of York's HQ, tel. 020/7823–2332) at the modern-art-focused Saatchi Gallery.

Albert Bridge Rd., SW11.
Tube: Sloane Sq.

020/8871-7530; www.wands
worth.gov.uk/parks

 Battersea Park, free; Battersea
Park Children's Zoo, £5.50
2-15, £6.50 ages 15 and up,
£26 family (2 adults, 2 kids)

 Daily 8 am–dusk

All ages

pond, this small and manageable zoo is especially child-friendly, with multiple opportunities to touch, encounter, and pet the animals (especially at feeding time).

After a walk through the butterfly garden, check out the park's Japanese Peace Pagoda (donated by Buddhist monks in 1985) and the well-equipped adventure playground, or think about hiring the park's distinctive half go-cart, three-wheel recumbent bicycles (tel. 020/7498-6543). They only take seconds to get the hang of, and once astride your kids will have a blast whizzing about.

Slow the pace down in the late afternoon with a stroll through the pretty Sub-Tropical Gardens in the southwestern tip of the park created by John Gibson in the 1860s with plants from his orchid-hunting days in India. There are boats for hire from Easter to September on the boating lake, which is beside a wooded idyll scattered with sculptures by Henry Moore and Barbara Hepworth.

MAKING THE MOST OF YOUR TIME Weekend and school activities at the Battersea Park Children's Zoo include seasonal events, face painting, animal mask-making workshops, and Mammal Detectives—where kids ages seven and up might have to solve the mystery of the stolen hazelnuts.

KEEP IN MIND The area that Battersea Park now covers was once known as Battersea Fields, and was known as a popular spot for dueling. At 8 am on Saturday March 21, 1829, the Prime Minister, the Duke of Wellington, and the Earl of Winchilsea met here in secret—near the Thames—to settle a matter of honor (a spat over the establishment of King's College, London, and the Catholic Relief bill). The Duke deliberately aimed his pistol wide, and the Earl fired his into the air. Earl Winchilsea later retracted, and wrote the Duke a full apology!

BOROUGH MARKET

67

Cured meats or caramels? Pork pies or oysters? Cheese plate or cheese toastie? Why choose? Come hungry and come early (and often!) is our best advice when it comes to all the food, glorious food, at bustling Borough Market off Borough High St. near London Bridge and Southwark Cathedral. It's a must-visit for foodies and a go-to for local chefs looking for the freshest and best ingredients for some of London's top restaurants.

Kids will feel like they've walked into Charlie's Chocolate Factory, except instead of chocolate rivers and crazy chewing gum, there are stalls filled with fresh baked breads, rare meats and cheeses, delicious hot pastries, candy, chocolates, and more. The chatter, buzz, colors, flavors, and fragrances are a delight for the senses and kids will love chasing from stall to stall for free samples.

First mentioned in 1276, housed under cavernous Victorian railway arches, and framed with exuberant wrought-iron work, more than 4½ million visitors a year swarm and cram this buzzy market for its head-swiveling cornucopia of 120-odd fruit and veg stalls, food stands, and specialist shops and purveyors, selling prime and hard-to-find produce from

EATS FOR KIDS

Line up at **Brindisa** (18–20 Southwark St., tel. 020/7357–8880) for the Alejandro chorizo rolls or nosh grilled scallops and bacon at **Shellseekers** fish stall in the Middle Market. Or try **Elliot's Cafe** (12 Stoney St., tel. 020/7403–7476) for kids' gourmet cheeseburgers and fried potatoes.

MAKING THE MOST OF YOUR TIME.

Besides the stalls, there's much to hold the kids' attention, like watching apple-pressing demos during themed events, listening to accordion shows, or stumbling across the market's resident chef whipping up a smashing meal, say, of new-season grouse, beetroot, and red wine sauce at the Demonstration Kitchen in the Jubilee Market (cooking demos generally take place between noon and 2 Thursday–Saturday). If things get a little hectic, steal away to look at the Shakespeare memorial, the stained glass, and the soaring Gothic arches at Southwark Cathedral, or find a quiet bench nearby.

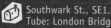 Southwark St., SE1.
Tube: London Bridge

 Free

 M–W 10–3, T 11–5, F 12–6, Sa 8–5

020/7407–1002; www.
boroughmarket.org.uk

All ages

across Britain and abroad. There's artisan cheeses and best-of-British fruit and veg; craft beers and local ciders; sourdough loaves and home-baked cakes; rare-breed meat and spicy chorizo; fresh fish, scallops, and oysters; plus truffle oil, pralines, paella, and tortillas. Not to mention a great bunch of nearby cafés, bars, restaurants, boutiques, and traditional English pubs.

The market is open for lunch on Monday to Wednesday (10–3), and on Thursday 11–5, Friday noon–6, and Saturday 8–5. Get here early, because it fills up fast and can get very crowded—especially on Friday and Saturday afternoon.

Start off wandering the covered stalls, encouraging young eaters to nibble any samples offered along the way. After picking up, say, some funky padrn peppers, fig balls, wild boar, or chili chipotle, refuel with curbside sizzling ostrich burgers, duck sandwiches, or hot Swiss raclette cheese, and then check out the whiff in the Neal's Yard truckle cheese shop (and Stilton specialists), the aromas in the Monmouth Coffee Co., and the *liddle* piggies lined up in the Ginger Pig butchers, before hitting a nearby café to sit, digest . . . and make room for dessert.

KEEP IN MIND Borough Market and its moody Dickensian environs and lockups have been featured in a number of films, including *Lock, Stock and Two Smoking Barrels* (1998), *Bridget Jones's Diary* (2001), and *Harry Potter and the Prisoner of Azkaban* (2004). The location where Harry Potter gets off the Knight Bus and enters the Leaky Cauldron under the railway bridge at No. 7 Stoney St., is in reality a flower shop called Chez Michele. Next door, at No. 8 Stoney St., was also the location for the Third-Hand Bookshop, a large used bookshop (supposedly on Charring Cross Rd.), where Harry met Gilroy Lockhart.

BRITISH LIBRARY

This is not a library where you can withdraw the latest Harry Potter (it's not a lending library at all, but rather for research); still, you can discover some absolutely *magical* things here. Take the redbrick building itself. It has a broad Mediterranean-style piazza entrance with an Anne Frank memorial tree, and inside, the white interior has staircases and escalators that lead to countless reading rooms. The library has a calm atmosphere, one that makes any child with an interest in reading want to investigate further.

A staggering 150 million items are held here, including 14 million books, nearly a million journals, 58 million patents, 3 million sound recordings, plus important manuscripts, music, maps, and stamps. The Sir John Ritblat Gallery brings some of these precious items to the public eye. You can listen to wonderful extracts from the library's sound archives, including the voice of Florence Nightingale, the Beatles' last tour interview, and Nelson Mandela's trial speech.

MAKING THE MOST OF YOUR TIME The Sir John Ritblat Gallery devotes a fascinating room to the Magna Carta—Latin for "Great Charter"—which was agreed at Runnymede in 1215 and sealed by King John after powerful barons rebelled and captured London. It outlined basic rights and the principles that no one was above the law, including the king. It charted the right to fair trial, and limits on taxation without representation, and later inspired other documents, like the US Constitution and Universal Declaration of Human Rights.

96 Euston Rd., NW1.
Tube: Euston, King's Cross

 Free; charge for special exhibitions

 020/7412-7332; www.bl.uk

 M and W–F 9:30–6, T 9:30–8, Sa 9:30–5, Su 11–5

10 and up

Check out the displays of notable letters written on thick, worn paper in browned ink, including one by Gandhi during his fast in 1943; Admiral Nelson's last letter to his lover Emma, along with a lock of his hair; and one in secret cipher written by Charles I during the English Civil War. Epic holdings on view include Magna Carta, the Lindisfarne Gospels, the Gutenburg Bible, Shakespeare's First Folio and manuscripts by Tolstoy, Honoré de Balzac, Virginia Woolf, and Jane Austen. Among the composers' scores, several inches thick, are creations by Handel and Bach—quite a contrast to the Beatles' felt-tip scribblings on scraps of paper. Some sacred texts have survived as fragments, on pieces of papyrus, cotton, and palm leaf. Kids can't touch the manuscripts, but they will love the Turning the Pages program, which lets you leaf virtually through books, such as Leonardo da Vinci's Notebooks, page by page. Towering in the center of the building is a six-story glassed-in column that houses the library of the bibliophile George III. It contains 65,000 books—a fitting heart to Britain's world-renowned and magnificent deposit library.

KEEP IN MIND
The British Library receives a copy of every publication produced in the UK and Ireland, and 3 million new items are incorporated every year. If you saw 5 items here each day, it would take you 80,000 years to see the whole collection!

EATS FOR KIDS The library's first-floor **King's Library** restaurant run by Peyton & Byrne is more of a cafeteria with self-service trays, offering imaginative soups, sandwiches, pastries, salads, pies, and stir-frys. As you munch, you can marvel at the leather, gold-lettered spines of books in George III's library (which was given to the nation in 1823). If it's sunny outside, relax in the piazza with a snack from **M&S Simply Food** on Euston Rd., or get kids' portions of cod and chips, hamburgers, or hot dogs at the stunning and ornate bar at the **Gilbert Scott** (tel. 020/7278-3888) **at St. Pancras.**

BRITISH MUSEUM

65

Walking through the towering colonnaded entrance and into the spectacular glass-domed Great Court, you may well feel as if you're visiting some great temple. That's not far from reality, as the museum is a shrine to objects from civilizations around the world and millions of years of history. Opened in 1759 with a collection of 71,000 objects bequeathed by naturalist and collector Sir Hans Sloane, the museum's permanent collection now includes 8 million objects—a collection so vast that you can barely scratch the surface in one visit. Before you come, check out the "Family visits" and "Kids discover" sections on the museum's website to plan your visit. On arrival, head to the Reading Room at the heart of the Great Court (regular readers have included Marx, Lenin, and Gandhi) and get kitted out with themed activity backpacks, multimedia guides, and free pamphlets with trails that guide you to famous or cool exhibits.

The mummies are always a popular choice, and in the Roxie Walker Galleries on the upper floor, attractive displays demystify the unusual rituals of the ancient Egyptians, including

MAKING THE MOST OF YOUR TIME Because of the museum's huge size, allow at least half a day for a first visit or, if possible, break up a full-day visit with some playtime at nearby Coram's Fields (#58). Sunday can be quite crowded. Late afternoon on Thursday or Friday is best to avoid the multitudes.

KEEP IN MIND Themed activity backpacks from the Families desk in the Great Court (available weekends and on school holidays, free with £10 deposit) include materials and tools to dress up as an ancient Greek, write your name in ancient hieroglyphs, build a winged lion, and make a mosaic. Kids can also avail of an audio tour of 58 objects (£3:50 for under-12s) and six "hands-on" tables where they can handle objects like pottery and coins. Look out for special family events—on topics like Shakespeare's London—most of which are free and drop-in, plus free half-day digital media workshops on everything from mummies to medieval creatures.

Great Russell St., WC1.
Tube: Holborn, Russell Sq.,
Tottenham Ct. Rd.

 Free

Museum Sa–Th 10–5:30, F 10–8:30;
Great Court Sa–Th 9–6, F 9–8:30

020/7323–8299; www.britishmuseum.org

4 and up

gruesome yet practical methods for preserving bodies. Nearby you can see the bust of Ramesses II from 1279 BC or the Rosetta Stone, which enabled experts to decode Egyptian hieroglyphs.

Brought to England in 1816 by Lord Elgin, the marble sculptures of Greek gods and warriors that lined the Parthenon in Athens 2,500 years ago are among the museum's greatest gems. (They're controversial, too, because Greece would *really* like them back.) In a side room, imaging wizardry shows how the riders in the fabled frieze might have looked; there's a special interactive section for kids.

You can discover the people who lived in Britain thousands of years ago, including an actual 1st-century AD example: Lindow Man, who was preserved in a peat bog in Cheshire. Close by is the Sutton Hoo haul of swords and helmets that may have belonged to Rædwald, king of East Anglia in the 7th century. Other sections of interest to kids include exhibits on early North Americans, including the headdress of Yellow Calf, as well as Aztec mosaics, the Lewis Chessmen, and the Royal Game of Ur from ancient Mesopotamia.

EATS FOR KIDS At the **Court Café** you can people-watch while munching on sandwiches and sticky patisserie. With repro Greek-battle wall friezes, the **Gallery Café** serves hot meals and salads, including kids' options. Opposite the main entrance, **Pizza Express** (30 Coptic St., tel. 020/7636–3232) has a streamlined Italian bistro setting; obliging staff and good-value pizza, pasta, and salads. Minimalist, canteen-style **Wagamama** (4 Streatham St., tel. 020/7323–9223), has kids' menus with filling noodle, fish, and rice dishes from £3 up.

BUCKINGHAM PALACE

Always wondered what the Queen's State Rooms at Buckingham Palace look like but too polite to ask her Majesty for a tour? Why not pop in and have a nose around the outrageously gold-leaf-and-bling-tastic world of Elizabeth II and the British monarchy while the Queen is away on her holidays at Balmoral Castle in Scotland.

Open for only a short period in July and August to October, you can tour 19 impossibly grand State Rooms at the Queen's official London residence, including the majestic Ball Room, the lavish White Drawing Room, and the regal Throne Room, where the Duke and Duchess of Cambridge (Prince William and Kate) had their famous formal wedding pictures taken ("Say 'Cheese,' Ma'am, *please!*"). Here, you'll see two empty thrones embroidered with "ER" and "P," which were used by Elizabeth II and the Duke of Edinburgh at the coronation in 1953.

Once known as Buckingham House (when it was owned by the Duke of Buckingham) and sold to George III for £28,000 in 1761, Buckingham Palace has been a royal residence

MAKING THE MOST OF YOUR TIME After you've seen how
the other half lives in the State Rooms, see how the other half travels at the Royal Mews
(#17) stables. Here, you'll find the fairy-tale Gold State Coach, almost completely gold with
cherubs and two mythical Tritons on the back to ward off interlopers. You can also admire
the open-topped 1902 State Landau carriage (used during the Queen's Diamond Jubilee
celebrations), inspect a fleet of Rolls-Royce Phantoms, and watch the 30-odd Cleveland
Bay and Windsor Grey carriage horses being fed, groomed, and put through their paces in
the 18th-century riding school.

Buckhingham Palace Rd., SW1A.
Tube: St James's Park, Victoria

020/7766-7300; www.
royalcollection.org.uk

 £10.25 ages 5–17; children under 5
free; £18 adults; £47 family tickets
(2 adults and 3 under-17s); £83
family "A Royal Day Out" tickets
(2 adults and 3 under-17s).

Open June 30–July 8 and July
31–Oct 7; 9:45–6 daily (last
admission 4)

 All ages

since a young Queen Victoria moved in in 1837, and it's grown over the years to an imposing 775 rooms, 52 Royal and guest bedrooms, and 78 bathrooms.

On this short tour, you'll pass Belle Époque and Chinese Regency–style rooms furnished with priceless Sévres porcelain, jewel cabinets, lavish crystal chandeliers, Canova sculptures and immaculate Canelettos, van Dycks, Rubens, Rembrandts, and Vermeers.

Three-in-one "A Royal Day Out" tickets gain entry to the adjacent Queen's Gallery, home to incredible art and treasures from the Royal Collection—such as drawings by Leonardo da Vinci and oils by Hans Holbein—as well as entry to the Royal Mews, where you can take a free 45-minute guided tour of the Queen's working stables and livery carriages—including the dazzling Gold State Coach, built for George III in 1762.

EATS FOR KIDS

Take tea, scones, or crown-topped cappuccinos at the Palace's **Garden Café** overlooking the royal gardens. Or the **Spaghetti House** (3 Bressenden Pl., tel. 020/7834–5650) serves excellent Italian pastas and pizza dishes in a friendly bistro setting, with smaller £5 portions available for kids.

KEEP IN MIND Strollers are not permitted, so ask for free baby carriers. Be sure to pick up audio guides and family activity bags, with puzzles, challenges, and games so kids won't be frustrated by the look-but-don't-touch nature of the tour. The refined 40-acre gardens—the largest private garden in London—provide a welcome outlet after the visit.

CHANGING THE GUARD

What photo memories of London are complete without a picture of a rifle-shouldered, stone-faced guard in his black bearskin cap and scarlet tunic? If you want to be photographed with a guard, head to Horse Guards Arch, Whitehall, and for full, foot-stomping pageantry, Buckingham Palace, the Queen's London home, is the place.

In summer, arrive by 11—or by 10:30 if you want a place by the gates—to stake a good vantage point at the palace. Just before 11:30 you can hear the bands' music, punctuated by shouted commands, as the sea of horses and red tunics winds down Birdcage Walk. It's a great sight, bringing traffic to a stop, and a rousing sound, too, with music from military marches to pop songs. This is the Queen's Guard, made up of the many different regiments of the Household Division, and it's the Foot Guards who exchange duty with a new guard, in a 45-minute ceremony known as Changing the Guard or Guard Mounting. On horseback is the cavalry, the Life Guards or the Blues and Royals, while on foot is a regiment of Grenadiers or Coldstream, Scots, Irish, or Welsh Guards. Among the dazzle of red, white, and gold you can pick out the different regiments. The Life Guards wear red tunics with

MAKING THE MOST OF YOUR TIME If the Palace gates are already crowded when you arrive, head to the Wellington Barracks on Birdcage Walk where the guard is inspected at 11 am before going to the Palace for the change ceremony. Few people know about it, so you can always get a good view.

KEEP IN MIND Originally granted to the Grenadiers for their role in the defeat of Napoleon's army at Waterloo, the signature furry bearskin cap is surprisingly light and it can last 100 years (which makes these caps a bargain at about £650 each). Although the Canadian black bear pelts are prone to moths and fire, they're preferred to synthetic copies with "fur" that stands alarmingly on end when the wearer is underneath an electrical tower. For more cool guard facts and to view dioramas and every kind of toy model soldier, visit the Guards Museum (Birdcage Walk, tel. 020/7414–3428), open daily 10–4; £5 ages 16 and up.

Buckingham Palace and Whitehall, SW1.
Tube: Victoria, Charing Cross

 020/7766-7300 Buckingham Palace,
020/7414-2479 Household Division;
www.royal.gov.uk

 Free

Buckingham Palace May–July, daily
11:30, check for times in fall and
winter; Horse Guards M–Sa 11, Su 10

All ages

white plumed helmets, and the Blues and Royals, blue with red plumed helmets. The Grenadiers'
bearskins have white plumes on one side. By day, the soldiers look the historical part in their
elaborate dress uniforms, but at night they patrol the palace grounds in combat kit. Occasionally, when the usual guard is on operational duty, you may see Commonwealth units. There is
no ceremony on very wet days, so call ahead if you can't tell a wet day from a very wet day!

Other guard mounting takes place at 11 daily (10 on Sunday) at Horse Guards Parade, where
the Life Guard leaves Hyde Park Barracks via Constitution Hill and the Mall to change duty.
Once Henry VIII's tournament ground, Horse Guards Parade is the setting for various military
ceremonies. Saturdays in June are especially active with rehearsals for the Trooping the
Colour—a vibrant display of pageantry held mid-June to mark the Queen's birthday. Tickets
for seated areas are available in advance by mail from the Household Division. At the
Tower of the London (#6), you can see 'Beefeaters' at the 700-year-old daily Ceremony of
the Keys at 9:30 pm if you obtain a pass in advance from the Tower. You can also spot
guards outside St. James's Palace, the offices of the Prince of Wales throughout the year.

EATS FOR KIDS North of Green Park, a few minutes' walk away,
the **Hard Rock Cafe** (150 Old Park La., tel. 020/7514–1700) bulges with
rock memorabilia, plays loud music, and does a great line in burgers as well as
£7.50 kids' menus for under-10s.

CHELSEA PHYSIC GARDEN

"The mandrake's cry is fatal to anyone who hears it," declares Hermione Granger in *Harry Potter and the Chamber of Secrets,* but hopefully you'll never really know if it's true because you're not allowed to pull up the mandrakes (gardeners let out an ungodly "scream" if you do) or unearth any of the other rare plants, flowers, or specimens at this enchanting hidden gem of a historic garden on the Thames in Chelsea, which was known as the Apothecaries' Garden when it opened in 1673.

Herbologists of all ages will revel in this seemingly secret redbrick walled garden and its well-laid-out collection of 5,000 edible, useful, medicinal, and historical plants, which was set up by the Worshipful Society of Apothecaries as a place to train (*budding?*) apprentices in identifying plants for medicinal and botanical purposes and recently revitalized to celebrate man's relationship with plants.

The garden is arranged thematically, so you can explore carnivorous specimens (an obvious first stop with kids) including sundews and Venus Flytraps, or wander through the Tropical Corridor, where you'll see vanilla pods and Spanish Moss. Perfume and aromatherapy bor-

MAKING THE MOST OF YOUR TIME You can sketch, paint and make models with twigs and leaves on the Art of Gardening kid's activity sessions, which are aimed at children aged four and up. Fives and over can pick up gardening tips, such as how best to grow and care for plants, take cuttings and plant seeds, while popular chocolate sessions begin with a tour of the garden, and end with a tasting session with staff from nearby Rococo Chocolates. Or kids can go home with syrup, ointments, and scented bags after a lotions and potions session, learning all about herbal medicine. Check online, and book ahead.

66 Royal Hospital Rd., SW3. Tube: Sloane Sq.

 £9 adults, £6 ages 5–15

020/7352–5646; www. chelseaphysicgarden.co.uk

 Open T–F 12–5; closed Sa; Su and bank holidays 12–6; Apr 1–Oct. 31: Tu–F, Su 11–6

 All ages

ders showcase everything from lemon verbena to lavender, redcurrants, and tomato leaves, and you'll find Madagascar periwinkle—a plant with anti-cancer properties, as well as meadowsweet—the basis of aspirin, in the Pharmaceutical garden. In the Useful Plants area you'll find burdock leaves that inspired Velcro, and sacred lotus plants that lie behind waterproof fabrics.

There's lichen dotted around the walls and benches, a pond full of damselflies, newts, tadpoles, and leeches, plus an early rockery (made from Icelandic lava and rocks from the Tower of London), beehives, and a monkey-puzzle tree.

Full- or half-day family activity days are a bargain at £6:50 or £5:50 and include brilliant garden tours and workshops, including lively sessions exploring chocolate, creepy crawlies, herbal medicine lotions and potions, garden photography, nature printing, and a session on CSI: Chelsea, an introduction to forensic biology.

KEEP IN MIND Botanist and "plant hunter" Sir Hans Sloane bought the Manor of Chelsea in 1712 and leased the garden to the Worshipful Society of Apothecaries for £5 a year in perpetuity and on condition that they supplied the Royal Society with 50 herbarium samples a year, up to a total of 2,000 plants. Sloane also had cotton sent from the garden to the new colony of Georgia in America in 1768, and a later curator, Robert Fortune, left for China in 1848 for the East India Company to collect tea to grow in India. A charity now runs the garden, and still pays only £5 a year rent.

EATS FOR KIDS
Admire gorgeous table-set pink peonies at the quaint **Tangerine Dream Café** (tel. 020/7349–6464) inside the Chelsea Physic Garden and enjoy lavender scones, gruyére tarts, and seasonal salads. Or head up to **Byron** (300 King's Rd., tel. 020/7352–6040) on King's Road for £6.50 kid's meals, including a burger, fries, and vanilla ice cream.

CHINATOWN

Chinatown is a vivid and exciting experience for all the family, and with the crowds, languages, smells, lanterns, colors, crispy ducks in windows, profusion of bamboo dim sum steamers, and cheap Chinese stalls and stores that seem to sell every imaginable knickknack—from intricate fans to embroidered silk Chinese slippers in (lucky) red and (even *luckier*) gold, Chinatown is also a vivid and exciting experience for all the senses.

London's Chinatown is only a small grid of historic streets south of SoHo, wedged tightly between Shaftesbury Avenue, Charing Cross Road and the north side of Leicester Square. With a concentration of 80-odd Cantonese, Mandarin, Dongbei, and Taiwanese restaurants, it's the culinary, cultural, and social focal point of London's 115,000-strong Chinese community, where every shop, bar, bakery, restaurant, and worker seems to be Chinese, and where even the street signs are in English and Mandarin.

Ever bustling by day and night, and festooned with red lanterns, Gerrard Street is Chinatown's main drag and epicenter, well worth a stroll to people-watch and to

KEEP IN MIND

The site of a former military training ground, Lord Gerrard first allowed houses to be built on Gerrard St. in 1685. Since then, the area has been home to a host of immigrant and/or dissolute groups, including French Huguenots, Jews, Maltese, and Italians, as well as radicals and writers.

MAKING THE MOST OF YOUR TIME

Don't be enticed by the touts outside a number of less-reputable restaurants in the area, and don't go expecting cutting-edge decor or anything less than brisk (make that brusque!) service if you do duck in for a quick bite or family meal. Most underpaid and overstretched Canonese or Mandarin staff will engage with and take a shine to polite kids, and some will show young children round the open-kitchen dim sum making stations, if they ask nicely!

Gerrard St., W1.
Tube: Leicester Sq. Piccadilly Circus

 Free

 Open daily

 020/7407-1002; www.
chinatownlondon.org

 All ages

peer in all the Chinese restaurants and all-day dim sum dives (some of which are more highly recommended than others).

Allow time to browse the souvenir stalls; kids will love the Hello Kitty pens and £1.50 paper dragons. Then, head to the New Loon Moon Chinese supermarket, where you'll find Chinese pears and broccoli, pak choi greens, and pineapple-sized pink dragon fruit.

You might spot Chinese chess masters playing in the street, and it's worth watching the Chinese ladies making delicate-looking dim sum in the open shop-front kitchens of tasty (and recommended!) dim sum specialists on Lisle St., such as Leong's Legends (tel. 020/7734-3380) or Beijing Dumpling (tel. 020/7287-6888). The crispy roast duck is made to a secret recipe at the famed Four Seasons (tel. 020/7494-0870) on Gerrard St., and it's worth squeezing into its carpeted ground floor to try half an aromatic duck with pancakes, seafood rice, Chinese greens, and a few pots of Chinese tea.

EATS FOR KIDS Try tapioca-rich lychee or green apple "bubble" teas and red bean grass jelly at the fresh-looking but tucked-away **Candy Café** (3 Macclesfield St., tel. 020/7434-4581), or enjoy old-school £9 set-meals including traditional sweet and sour pork or chicken in oyster sauce at **Mr Kong's** (21 Lisle St., tel. 020/7437-4371).

CHURCHILL WAR ROOMS

During World War II, this warren of rooms below the government offices of Whitehall was the nerve center of military operations. Prime Minister Winston Churchill, along with the most important people in the military and government, worked and slept in this secret bunker while the German Luftwaffe bombed the streets above. Today you can tour these historic rooms, some preserved exactly as they were when the war ended in 1945. It's as if time stood still—literally. The clocks all read two minutes to five, and background sounds include wailing sirens, ringing phones, voices, footsteps in the corridors, and the tap-tap of busy typewriters. It makes for an eerie atmosphere but an informative visit.

A free audio guide explains about daily life from room to room. You can see top-secret places, including the tiny room—a converted broom closet—in which Churchill made frequent phone calls to President Roosevelt. The Map Room is probably the most compelling, because you get a real sense of the theater of war. Every pin, page, book, map, and even sugar cube remains as it was in the height of activity, when Churchill and his top military brass plotted troop movements across the world.

EATS FOR KIDS The walls of the museum's **Switch Room Café** are lined with photos of a devastated London during wartime bombing. Blitz your taste buds with a £9.65 taco lunch with quesadillas at **Texas Embassy Cantina** (1 Cockspur St., off Trafalgar Sq., tel. 020/7925–0077). Kids will also find burgers, burritos, hot dogs, key lime pie, and refill sodas at this lively rancho-themed eatery.

Clive Steps, King Charles St., SW1.
Tube: Westminster, Exit 6

 £16:50 ages 16 and up

 Daily 9:30–6; last admission 5

 020/7930–6961; www.iwm.org.uk

8 and up

Churchill was a formidable presence, a remarkable politician and leader, and a prolific writer, and in an annex of the War Rooms, a museum has been devoted to the life of the man behind the iconic image. Video clips and interactive displays allow you to explore Churchill's life in different chapters, from schoolboy Winston to maverick politician, sentimental husband, and Nobel Prize–winning writer, to orator and Prime Minister before, during, and after the War. Kids should make a beeline for the touch-screen timeline where they will discover Churchill's life, work, and achievements through personal stories, facts, letters, and even school reports. This comprehensive homage exposes a larger-than-life man, flaws and all, and helps you to understand how and why one man toiled to change the course of history for better . . . and in many ways succeeded.

KEEP IN MIND
Keep your eyes open in the kitchen and you might see a mousetrap. Mice (and rats, too) were regular visitors below ground, and to help control these unwelcome guests, Churchill took in a stray cat, naming it after another great leader: Nelson.

MAKING THE MOST OF YOUR TIME Museum staff
will sometimes "open the box" to allow kids to try on military berets, tin air-raid warden hats, and regulation gas masks; such sessions are unscheduled but worth asking about. Quiz trails and free audio guides (available at admissions) will keep kids engaged, while older kids can test their skills at solving clues via the computer games and multimedia monitors dotted around the museum.

COLUMBIA ROAD FLOWER MARKET

"There's no finer way to spend a Sunday morning in London than exploring the famous Columbia Road flower market in the East End—a riot of colorful cut flowers, plants, shrubs, herbs, bulbs, and trees set in a narrow 1860s Dickensian cobbled street surrounded by 60-odd independent and quirky shops, workmen's cafés, bric-a-brac merchants, vintage stores, antique dealers, pubs, delis, restaurants, galleries, and studios.

"Everyfin' a fivah!" or *"Twoo for a tennah!!"* are a couple of the bellowing Cockney stall-holders' market refrains, as they theatrically outdo each other for your attention, creating a scene that is a bit of a cross between *Mary Poppins, Oliver,* and *My Fair Lady.* Kids love the East End Cockney banter almost as much as shopping (and sniffing) the buckets of bargain-priced flowers and trays of plants and herbs on the 52 market stalls; let them loose with a camera here and you might just trigger a passion for photography, or at least, you'll have some beautiful bloom-filled photos for the family album.

MAKING THE MOST OF YOUR TIME The flower market starts at 8 on Sunday morning, and lasts only until 3. If you're buying flowers, come early for the best pick, just after 8, or, if you're looking for a bargain, start buying at around 2, when the stallholders start to off-load the last of their perishable stock.

EATS FOR KIDS The nostalgic century-old Jones Dairy (23 Ezra St., tel. 020/7739–5372), a former stable, offers a charming retro decor with family-friendly Welsh cakes, pasties, and rolls as well as fry-ups and smoked salmon bagels with cream cheese. Enjoy bagels or salt beef and rye bread "sarnies" at family-run **Café Columbia** (138 Columbia Rd., tel. 020/7033–8764), or delicious shepherd's pie or English fish-and-chips at **Albion** (2–4 Boundary St., tel. 020/7729–1051).

Columbia Rd., E2.
Tube: Old St.

 Free

Su 8–3

www.columbiaroad.info

All ages

It was a remarkable Victorian philanthropist and friend of Charles Dickens, Baroness Burdett-Coutts, who established Columbia Road market in 1869 as a covered market for 400 stalls on a former watercress field and near a notorious slum. The market was later moved outdoors, and from Saturday to Sunday trading (because most stallholders were Jewish). These days, locally grown or imported from Holland, the flowers, naturally, change with the seasons, but you'll find cracking great bunches of gladioli, lilies, chrysanthemum, amaryllis, tulips, peonies, roses, and pussy willow. There are herbs from purple sage to Moroccan mint, bluebells, iris and daffodil bulbs, and shrubs ranging from olive and citrus to 10-foot-high bamboo trees.

Once you've been up and down a few times, now's a good time to explore the Indie shops and bric-a-brac yards. After all the pretty inedibles at the flower market, kids will hyperventilate at retro sweet shop Suck and Chew (tel. 020/8983-3504), where they can fill red-and-white striped paper bags with sweets like fizz balls, acid drops, and sherbet fountains.

KEEP IN MIND Shoreditch is home to a gazillion trendy artists and creatives, so—when in Rome—it's worth popping into Seamus Ryan's (7 Ezra St., tel. 020/7613–1560) nearby studio. Members of the public are invited to be photographed each Sunday (10–3) as part of Ryan's ongoing photography project, known as Sunday Shots. Every session has a different theme or backdrop, and you can see his distinctive photos of yourselves a few days later online. It's free, and kids love it.

CORAM'S FIELDS

"*No Adults Unless accompanied by a child*" says the sign at the entrance to Coram's Fields, a unique 7-acre walled garden park in historic Bloomsbury and a fun-filled haven for kids. It's appropriate that kids take priority here (even if the sign is for safety reasons) as Coram Fields sits on the site of the former and famous London Foundling Hospital for "exposed and deserted young children," established by philanthropist Captain Thomas Coram. The hospital was sold and demolished in 1926, but campaigners like press baron Lord Rothermere fought successfully to keep the site as a children's park, which eventually reopened as Coram's Fields in 1939.

Today, the Children's Centre provides free child care for 2–5-year-olds for 48 weeks a year, and there's a daily free (or £2) drop-in program for under-5s, such as soft play days, DiDi Dancing, or 45-minute Little Kickers soccer sessions—perfect for visiting kids looking for local playmates. During school holidays, 6–16-year-olds can join free street dance sessions, bleep tests, or mini-soccer tournaments between noon and 4, and there are

EATS FOR KIDS The Austrian **Kipferl Cafe** inside the park, offers sausages, pasta, and sandwiches and is open March–November, 10–5. Head outside for family-run Italian **Ciao Bella** (tel. 020/7242–4119) on trendy Lamb's Conduit Street, which does kids' half-portions of pasta for £5 (apart from seafood) and also has fine pizza. In the nearby Brunswick Centre, **Giraffe** (tel. 020/7812–1336) has fish fingers, burgers, or popcorn chicken for under £6, and **Carluccio's** has £6.50 kids' meals, with grissini, ravioli, lasagna, and tubs of gelato ice cream.

93 Guilford St., WC1.
Tube: Russell Sq.

 Free

Daily 9–dusk

020/7837–6138; www.corams
fields.org

All ages

regular sports drop-in sessions 4 pm–5 pm for dodgeball, touch rugby, trampolining, athletics, and cricket.

The park's facilities include big tunneled slides, swings, spinners, a flying fox, Olympic-sized paddling pool in summer, a couple of sand pits, and a natural play area. At the adventure playground you'll find climbing equipment galore (all made from natural materials), plus a wood-chip floor, and an aerial zip-wire, which is extremely popular with kids. Nearby are all-weather sports pitches, a drop-in nursery, plus a city farm with goats, ducks, rabbits, chickens, and sheep.

MAKING THE MOST OF YOUR TIME Be sure to stroll up Lamb's Conduit Street on your way out. You'll find a quaint cluster of alfresco cafés and Indie shops running south of the park. Look out for small imprint Persephone Books or charming children's bookshop, the Lamb Bookshop, known for its remarkably good range of books and toys.

KEEP IN MIND Captain Thomas Coram achieved great success in the New World with his shipwright's business in Boston and Taunton, Massachusetts. When he retired to London, he was appalled by the sight of dead and dying babies abandoned in the streets. Enlisting the support of George II and Queen Caroline, and political figures like Horace Walpole and artist William Hogarth, Coram eventually received a royal charter to establish the Foundling Hospital in 1739.

COURTAULD GALLERY

57

When it comes to art museums, small is beautiful, especially with children. The compact nature of this gallery is one of its chief assets, making it easy to navigate and manageable for kids, and the swell setting and many magnificent paintings provide a visual feast.

The prettiest approach to the gallery is from the river, by the steps on Waterloo Bridge, and past the impressive 18th-century neoclassical buildings that make up the whole of Somerset House (#12). Head across the cobbled courtyard to the gallery entrance. In 1779, the gallery rooms housed the Royal Academy of Arts, which later moved to Burlington House, in Piccadilly, in 1867. If you look up at the decorative plasterwork ceilings, you can still see the curly RA initials. The rooms have had a makeover, but the main reason for coming is to see monumental works by Impressionists and Post-Impressionists.

To help kids get the most out of the Courtauld, pick up a gallery guide at the admission desk. Covering the gallery's key paintings and giving a neat art-history tour, the

EATS FOR KIDS

A short walk along the Strand, the long-standing American family entertainment restaurant, **Smollensky's** (105 Strand, tel. 020/7497–2101), has games, goodie bags, and balloons. The kids' menu is a crowd-pleaser—with cheeseburgers, fish fingers, chocolate pie, and "kids cocktails." (See also Somerset House, #12.)

MAKING THE MOST OF YOUR TIME Plunge kids into the world of painting through family workshops held on Saturday during school holidays. These sessions allow children to look closely at an artist or style and then produce their own mini masterpieces—perhaps looking at self-portraits influenced by van Gogh or fabric-pen designs created after looking for textile patterns in paintings. Workshops cost £12–£15 and last four or more hours.

Somerset House, Strand, WC2.
Tube: Covent Garden, Holborn

 £6 adults; free M 10–2
(except holidays)

 Daily 10–6; last admission 5:30

020/7848-2526; www.
courtauld.ac.uk

5 and up

booklet begins, appropriately, at the beginning with Lucas Cranach the Elder's *Adam and Eve*, an early narrative painting from 1526 that captures the moment Eve hands Adam an apple from the tree of knowledge. The trail then romps through another 100 years to the genius of the great Flemish and Dutch Baroque painters and their enchanting portraits and land-scapes, before leaping to the museum's collection of some of the finest Impressionist and Post-Impressionist paintings in the world. It's a breathless tour of art styles.

If you'd rather go straight to the Impressionist gems, head up the winding marble stair-case. Here you'll find world-class beauties like van Gogh's *Self-Portrait with Bandaged Ear*, Degas's *Two Dancers on Stage*, Manet's *A Bar at the Folies-Bergère*, or Renoir's *La Loge*. And look out: it's not unusual to find children sprawled on the floor while they draw intently.

KEEP IN MIND You can OD on art by visiting the Courtauld Gallery for free on Monday 10–2 (except bank holidays) and then strolling five minutes down the Strand to the (free) National Gallery and National Portrait Galleries at Trafalgar Square, before catching the 88 bus from there to the (free) Tate Britain art gallery in Pimlico, where you can get your fill of Turners, Constables, and Gainsboroughs.

COVENT GARDEN

Once notorious for its rowdy drinking dens and bawdy theater district, today's Covent Garden is instead known for its lively and vibrant markets and theatrical street performers, and is a magnet for locals and visitors alike. From its epicenter—the cobbled piazza and its covered market—to the surrounding streets, Covent Garden offers a cacophony of trendy shops, theaters, pubs, and eateries galore . . . though, you may have a little trouble dragging the kids away from some of London's coolest street shows!

The original walled "convent garden" was tended by monks in medieval times to provide produce for Westminster Abbey. Fruit, veg, and flower stalls thrived on the site from the mid-17th century until steel-and-glass halls were built in the 19th century. The market was threatened by developers in the 1970s but it survived and was restored to house a multitude of shops and terrace cafés. The quaint Apple Market has craft stalls and fashion boutiques, and West End divas sing alfresco arias in the Southern courtyard. The Jubilee Hall market is more of a souk, offering T-shirts and trinkets. Elsewhere, you can find

MAKING THE MOST OF YOUR TIME Weekends in mid-July, you might catch world-class performers from the nearby Royal Opera House delivering free abridged opera, dance, and music performances in the northeast corner of the piazza. The Royal Opera House hosts free lunchtime recitals on Monday featuring rising stars. Tickets are free but in demand, so reserve online (www.roh.org.uk/recitals/lunchtime-recitals) nine days before the concert date.

Covent Garden Piazza and Central Market, WC2.
Tube: Covent Garden

 Free

Piazza daily 24 hrs; Jubilee Market Hall T–F
9:30–6; Apple Hall M–Sa 10–7:30, Su 12–6,
some shops and restaurants much later

0870/780–5001 Covent Garden Central
Market; www.coventgardenlondonuk.com

 All ages

everything from Benjamin Pollock's Toyshop (tel. 020/7379–7866) for nostalgic Victorian paper theaters, to the world's largest Apple Store (tel. 020/7447–1400).

The only building remaining from the square's original 17th-century Italianate design is St. Paul's, the actors' church, whose interior is dotted with great performers' plaques (look for Charlie Chaplin's). In front on the piazza is *the* street theater hot spot, where kids will be mesmerized by acrobatics, magic, mimes, puppet shows like Punch and Judy, and can hear global musicians the likes of Chinese groups with melodious strings and exotic box instruments and Andean percussion ensembles.

The grand old entrance to the Royal Opera House (#15) is still on Bow Street, but there's a sleek new entrance off the piazza. Step inside and enjoy the soaring spaces, particularly the restored Floral Hall, formerly a storeroom for stage props and, before that, a 19th-century flower market.

KEEP IN MIND

In 1662, diarist Samuel Pepys noted that he had enjoyed an Italian puppet play here—the best he ever saw, and probably the first Mr. Punch show. For nearly 40 years, the annual May Fayre has celebrated this theatrical event in the garden of St. Paul's, where more than 30 gaily-striped Punch and Judy booths stage performances on the second Sunday in May.

EATS FOR KIDS **Masala Zone** (48 Floral St., tel. 020/7379–0101) dangles Rajastani puppets along with cheap culinary delights like chicken naan bread wraps or vegetable thalis for £4.85. Ever-reliable French chain **Cte** (17–21 Tavistock St., tel. 020/7379–9991) has kids-meals like sausage, mash, and carrots for £4.95. Chef Raymond Blanc's **Brasserie Blanc** (tel. 020/737–0666) overlooks the piazza and offers kids portions like beef Stroganoff for £6. Or slide into a booth at cool Jewish joint **Miskin's** (25 Catherine St., tel. 020/7240–2078) for half-sized salt beef or Reuben-on-rye sandwiches, meatballs, and mac-and-cheese.

CUTTY SARK

Walk the decks, hold, and beneath the gleaming copper-bottomed hull of this beautiful tea clipper, and you'll step into Britain's glorious merchant maritime past. Resplendent with its 152-foot mast and rigging—one of London's most iconic sights—the *Cutty Sark* has been raised 10 feet (following a fire and restoration) to reveal the elegant lines of her hull that enabled her reach the record-breaking speed of 17½ knots (20 mph) from Sydney to London. The last of the clippers that endured high seas and heavy weather to ferry tea from China, you can breathe in the smoky aroma of Lapsang Souchong tea absorbed over the years as you board.

The history of the ship, launched in 1869, is told in lively interactive displays and videos. In its glory days, the *Cutty Sark* (Scots for "short shirt" or "nightshirt") sliced through the seas and set record journey times to the other side of the world. When her cargo changed from tea to wool and thus her route from China to Australia, she could dash off the voyage to Sydney in a record 77 days, overtaking the mail steamship.

KEEP IN MIND

Wear grippy shoes to negotiate the many steep, narrow steps. And leave bags and backpacks at home.

EATS FOR KIDS For light bites, there's the museum café directly below the shiny copper hull. Or follow the seafaring theme at the wood-paneled, 18th-century Trafalgar Tavern (6 Park Row, tel. 020/8858–2909). This spot was a favorite haunt of Charles Dickens and government ministers who traveled downriver from Westminster to feast on specialty "whitebait dinners" (a tiny white fish), which was caught locally. Children's £7.50 options here include sausage and mash, cheeseburgers, and fish-and-chips. French-style Café Rouge (30 Stockwell St., tel. 020/8293–6660) serves a kid-size main course with dessert and drink for £6.25. Choices include cheese pancakes, pasta, or salmon with peas.

King William Walk, Greenwich, SE10.
Tube: Cutty Sark DLR

 £12 ages 16 and up, £6.50 ages 6–15, £29 family (2 adults, 2 children)

 Daily 10–5; last entry at 4, timed tickets

020/8312-6608; www.rmg.co.uk

4 and up

You can explore the Main and 'Tween Decks, plus the Lower Hold, Dry Dock, and Sammy Ofer gallery, which houses the ships' figureheads and has a glass ceiling directly beneath the hull. On the Main Deck, officers' and crew accommodations have been restored—all shiny wood and authentic fittings. The Master's mahogany saloon is the most luxurious; note the hanging tray that holds wineglasses secure. For the crew, accommodation was spare; peer in on a waxwork crew at ease in their quarters. Above deck is a wonderful web of rigging that totals 11 miles.

Below at the 'Tween Deck and Lower Hold, check out the cargo and storage, and find out if you pass muster as a sailor by pulling the weighted blocks for hoisting the sails, but first feel the strength of the sail section by the stairs. Imagine it being wet from storm and spray, increasing its weight fivefold. On weekends and holidays, wannabe salty dogs can learn rope knotting, sing and dance sea shanties, steer the wheel, and imagine themselves on a trade journey to Shanghai as costumed actors play captain and crew of this indomitable 963-ton ship. To rest your weary sea legs, try getting in a hammock without falling off—then imagine trying to sleep in one aboard a rocking and rolling ship.

MAKING THE MOST OF YOUR TIME After
exploring *Cutty Sark*, you'll also be suitably attired to wander around the winding Georgian village streets and the covered Greenwich Market on College Approach (it sells crafts, antiques, and tasty goodies), or to explore part of the Thames Path, which has great riverside views. Allow a day in Greenwich, as there's much to see, including Greenwich Park (#50), the National Maritime Museum (#27), and the Royal Observatory (#16). The Discover Greenwich tourist center near the *Cutty Sark* is a great starting point for orienting your day.

DENNIS SEVERS' HOUSE

54

Ring the old-fashioned doorbell, step over the threshold and into what feels like a rich and atmospheric Old Master painting or period theatrical set. Part time capsule and part art installation, this Georgian house in the Spitalfields neighborhood of the City offers a hauntingly magical historical experience, and a very physical sense of the past, as you explore—in complete silence—the candlelit chambers, ante rooms, corridors, and interrupted life of an 18th-century home.

Named for the late artist who created this extraordinary home for his own enjoyment (and donated it to the public), Dennis Severs lived in his time-capsule home without electricity or modern comforts so that he could capture the *exact* mood and experience of its 18th-century occupants. He even invented a fictional family of Huguenot silk merchants, the Jervis family, and created evocative still-life dramas and tableaux that conjure the rise and fall of the family's fortunes from 1724 to 1914.

As you make your way silently through the 10 rooms of the home, on the trail of the fictitious Jervis family who it seems have just left the room, your senses sharpen. You hear

EATS FOR KIDS **Leon** (3 Crispin Pl., tel. 020/7247–4369) has meatballs, fish fingers, or falafel with brown rice, peas, and lemonade for £2.99. Nearby kid experts **Giraffe** (Spitalfields Market, tel. 020/3116–2000) has cottage pie with broccoli or sausage, beans and mash for £4.25. Retro Cockney fish-and-chips purveyors **Poppies** (6–8 Hanbury St., tel. 020/7247–0892) has cod bites, fishcakes, or sausage-and-chips kids' meals for £4.95, and you can also learn Cockney rhyming slang from the wallpaper.

 18 Folgate St., E1.
Tube: Liverpool St.

 M 12–2; W 6–9 from Oct 1–Mar 31, timed tickets; S 12–4; twice monthly July–Nov

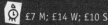 £7 M; £14 W; £10 S

 020/7247–4013; www.dennis severshouse.co.uk

9 and up

footsteps, muffled laughter. Fire crackles in the grate, and candles flicker. A clock chimes. There's a waft of cinnamon. As you walk the creaky wooden floorboards, you'll see fresh broken bread and a plate of half-eaten oysters on the kitchen table. There's red wine in the glasses, a silver tea pot, a wig, a quilled nib, pomegranates and grapes piled high, sugared almonds, and correspondence on the table.

In the Baroque and overflowing piano noble entertaining room, you'll be transfixed by a rococo mix of Georgian silks, drapes, oil paintings, china, and silverware. In the bedroom, there's a sumptuous red organza four-poster, which looks recently vacated. In the garret at the top of the house, it seems a family of six lodgers are living in these cramped, stripped quarters. You'll see their crumpled bedclothes, children's shoes on the floor, and smell a plate of cut onions.

The unique experiential tour takes about 45 minutes, but it requires restraint and quiet, so is perhaps best suited to older children.

MAKING THE MOST OF YOUR TIME Though it is still
considered off-the-beaten tourist track, this experience has become quite popular with nontourists. Book your visit by phone or online in advance; be prepared to indicate a preferred date and time of arrival, and a second choice. A typical visit lasts about 45 minutes.

KEEP IN MIND
This area gained its historic association with the silk industry after thousands of French Protestant Huguenot refugees sought sanctuary here, setting up thriving silk weaving ateliers in the early Georgian townhouses of Spitalfields.

FAT TIRE'S ROYAL LONDON BIKE TOUR

Your two feet can only take you so far when it comes to hitting London's many Royal sites, so why not equip them with two wheels—or even better, three—and a kid-friendly tour guide, and pedal your way through a fun royal agenda of parks, palaces, and parliaments, filled with tidbits about kings, queens, and princesses. Whether your own agenda is to hit all the city's highlights in one afternoon or just to expend a little kid energy on a beautiful day, Fat Tire Bike Tours' Royal London tour provides a great overview of the city, and an altogether much more satisfying and local-feeling experience than sitting on a cheesy tourist-bus.

Known for their comfy fat-tired, Californian "beach cruisers," family-friendly bike choices that include tandem and kid-size, top tour specialists Fat Tire Bike Tours offer small groups of about 12–15 cyclists, led by passionate and knowledgeable tour guides. The Royal London tour is about four hours but there's no need to bust out the yellow jersey; there are stops every 10 minutes or so for photo ops or to hear some history or anecdote outside a famous royal landmark.

KEEP IN MIND
Central London is pretty flat, so none of these tours are going to feel like the Tour de London. If taking a tour with younger kids, be sure to book tandem bikes, kid-size bikes (20-inch wheels) and youth bikes (24-inch wheels) in advance.

EATS FOR KIDS
You won't enter any landmarks along the tour, but if you want to eat before or after the tour, you can share the signature lobster noodle dish with ginger and onion sauce at famed Chinese **Mandarin Kitchen** (14–16 Queensway, tel. 020/7727–9012) opposite Queensway tube. Head into the National Portrait Gallery's **Portrait Café** (2 St. Martin's Pl., tel. 020/7312–2465) for mozzarella toasted sandwiches or ham frittatas (£4) at the top of Trafalgar Square. Or venture farther north to **Wahaca** (66 Chandos Pl., tel. 020/7240–1883) near Covent Garden for Mexican corn on the cob, courgette and cactus tacos, and chicken tostadas for under £10.

Look for Fat Tire's guide and sign outside Queensway Tube station; Tube: Queensway

 0788/2338-779; www.fattirebiketours.com

 £20 adults; £18 children; £10 tandem; child seat free

 Jan 1–Feb 28: M, Th, F, Sa, Su 11; Mar 1–May 14: 11 daily; May 15–Sept 15: 11 and 3:30; Sept 16–Nov 30: 11.

 10 and up

From the boardwalk in Kensington Gardens you'll see the elegantly revamped Kensington Palace (Prince William and Kate's London abode) and leisurely pass a 5-star hit-parade of landmarks like the Mall, Buckingham Palace, St James's Palace, Horse Guards Parade, Admiralty Arch, the Houses of Parliament, Big Ben, Westminster Abbey, 10 Downing St., and Trafalgar Square. The company has a rare license with the Royal Parks, so the majority of this tour is on quiet cycle lanes and on trails within well-tended and beautiful Royal Parks, such as Kensington Gardens, Hyde Park, Green Park, and St James's Park.

Fat Tire also has a popular five-hour River Thames bike tour, which takes in highlights like St Paul's Cathedral (#10), Shakespeare's Globe (#13), Tower Bridge, the Tower of London (#6), and Covent Garden (#56). This is suitable for over-12s, and ends with a Thames boat ride back to Westminster.

MAKING THE MOST OF YOUR TIME

You should arrive at meeting points 15 minutes before departure. Dress for English weather—that is, there's always a "chance of showers!" Fat Tire provides free helmets for all sizes, lightweight rain ponchos (if necessary), and gloves (for sale). Insurance is included in the price. During winter (December–February), they do five Royal Tours per week, so check availability.

FOUNDLING MUSEUM

When shipbuilder and sea captain Thomas Coram returned from sea in 1719, he was appalled to find children abandoned to the streets of London at the alarming rate of over a thousand a year. Coram campaigned relentlessly to build a refuge for these victims and in 1739 he was granted a royal charter to establish the London Foundling Hospital for the "maintenance and education of exposed and deserted children." Although the original building no longer exists, you can discover the poignant story of Britain's first home for abandoned children, its influential patrons, and London's first public art gallery, at this charming museum overlooking leafy Coram's Fields (#58).

Coram petitioned the good, the wealthy, and the artistic to help establish the hospital. Artist William Hogarth was one of the first governors of the hospital and a diligent bene-factor, donating his portrait of Thomas Coram to the hospital. As more artists donated works, the Foundling Hospital became a fashionable center of cultural display and the capital's first public art gallery. Paintings by such leading artists as Sir Joshua Reynolds and Thomas Gainsborough are today housed in fully restored interiors—just as they

MAKING THE MOST OF YOUR TIME Entry is free for accom-panying adults if you're going for Family Fun days (check Web for dates), where kids make Foundling-related postcards, and artwork linked to Handel, Dickens, and Hogarth. Kids will also enjoy dressing up in Foundling shoes and historical clothing in the ballroom. Be sure to try a bowl of Victorian "gruel" in the Museum Café.

40 Brunswick Sq., WC1.
Tube: Russell Sq.

 £7.50 ages 16 and up

Tu–Sa 10–5, Su 11–5

 020/7841-3600; www.
foundlingmuseum.org.uk

 4 and up

would have been seen by visitors to the hospital in the 1700s. Children can plug into the music of composer George Frideric Handel in a cozy room dedicated to the Foundling's famous patron. Handel held fund-raising concerts in the hospital's chapel and bequeathed the score of his great oratorio *Messiah* to the hospital.

The ground-floor exhibition tells of the persistence of Captain Coram in realizing his vision to create a haven for the care and education of these abandoned children. Sadly, there was limited space in the hospital and places were awarded by lottery for disease-free kids. The lucky ones were given a fresh start and new names. Mothers often left a token—like a thimble, a button, a poem, a hairpin, or a ribbon—by which they could identify their children, if they ever returned to reclaim them. Kids can trace the life story of a foundling through artifacts, oral testimonies, and photos . . . and will certainly leave counting their blessings!

EATS FOR KIDS
Make sure to indulge in some of the most delicious traditional cakes, tea, coffee, and hot chocolate in the **Foundling Museum Café**. The kids' lunch menu includes cheese toasties or chicken sandwiches for £3.70. When it's dry, you can take a table outside overlooking the leafy square.

KEEP IN MIND Next door to the museum, the associated Coram children's charity continues the old hospital's work with vulnerable kids. Enclosed by the colonnades of the old hospital building, Coram's Fields has swings, playgrounds, child care, and an animal enclosure with goats and sheep. Another Coram connection, Handel House Museum (25 Brook St., W1, tel. 020/7495–1685), has been re-created in Georgian style as the setting for concerts and a busy children's program.

GOLDEN HINDE

Get on board, me hearties! After spanning the globe and sailing more than 140,000 miles, the *Golden Hinde* has come to rest along the Thames. The galleon on the South Bank is not the famous 16th-century man-of-war captained by privateer Sir Francis Drake, however. That one rotted long ago. Instead, a beautiful handcrafted replica, docked between Southwark Cathedral and Shakespeare's Globe (#13), acts as a living museum. When at sea, its small crew lives very much like Drake's men did. Life was hard, and the men were tough, as you'll discover on this voyage into the past.

The info sheet for a self-guided tour details the parts of the ship and helps you sort out the mizzen from the mainmast and foremast. Better still is a tour with guides in Tudor dress (book ahead). Either way, between the masts and the bowels of the ship, you can explore five decks. The poop deck, for instance, held the only private cabin—the captain's. (The crew slept among pigs, chickens, and sheep, which were kept for food.)

EATS FOR KIDS

Keep scurvy at bay with soups, tartines, and salads, from **Le Pain Quotidien** (15 Winchester Walk, tel. 020/3657–6927). On Thursday (11–5), Friday (12–6) and Saturday (8–5) foodie haven **Borough Market** (Southwark St., tel. 020/7407–1002) has all the makings of a family-friendly picnic.

MAKING THE MOST OF YOUR TIME
You can book monthly "sleepover" living-history nights on the *Golden Hinde* (£43, not in winter), during which kids ages six and up (accompanied by an adult) can dress, sleep (bring a sleeping bag), eat, work, and man the guns as part of Drake's crew. If you can't stay overnight, try one of the three-hour daytime summer workshops on pirates, Sir Francis, or Tudors offered when school is out. Check the website for details.

1–2 Pickfords Wharf, Clink St., SE1.
Tube: London Bridge

 £6 ages 16 and up; £4.50
children 4–15; £18 family

 020/7403-0123; www.
goldenhinde.com

Daily: times vary, check online

6 and up

In the main deck's armory, you can try turning the capstan to haul the anchor. On the gun deck (painted red to camouflage bloodstains), you may get a chance to load the cannon and see it fire. By the way, if a lowly shipmate was found somewhere he shouldn't have been, punishment was severe. If he stole food, for example, his hand was nailed to the mast; after a few hours, the hand would probably have had to be chopped off. Among Drake's 80-strong crew of musicians, cooks, blacksmith, and minister, there was a barber surgeon, who performed amputations—with only alcohol as painkiller.

Watch your head while descending the ladders to the lower decks; headroom is minimal to keep the boat's center of gravity low. Here you'll find the bilge, where rocks stabilized the ship; food-storage barrels; and the galley, where meals—including salted and dried beef, beans, prunes, currants, and sea biscuits, often with maggots and other creepy crawlies—were prepared. Food for thought: with all this, how were Drake's men so victorious at sea?

KEEP IN MIND Young boys on the crew worked hard. One of their tasks was to carry the gunpowder for the guns. The boys were called powder monkeys because they climbed up and down the ladders from the lower deck to the gun deck as fast as their bent, monkeylike legs could carry them. When off duty, powder monkeys slept on the deck floor (with mouths shut to prevent animal waste from sloshing into their mouths!) in the same set of ragged clothes.

GREENWICH PARK

Flanked by the River Thames, and one of the largest green spaces in southeast London, Greenwich Park boasts the honor of being the oldest enclosed Royal Park. It also boasts the Greenwich Meridian line, a child-friendly boating lake, a maritime museum, urban sanctuary, and spectacular views, among other highlights.

Henry VIII hunted deer and wild boar in the 183-acre park, and he and his daughters, Mary and Elizabeth, were born in Greenwich Palace. The palace was eventually demolished, and the great architects Sir Christopher Wren and Sir John Vanbrugh built the Royal Naval Hospital for Queen Mary from 1696. It later became the Royal Naval College. These grand English Baroque buildings on the river, which include two domed structures with an open court between them, set the tone for a historical walk across the park.

St. Mary's Gate, by the *Cutty Sark* (#55) and past the Discover Greenwich visitor center, is a good place to start, as it takes you directly along the avenue to the heart and highest point of the park. From here you can take in the park's most beautiful panorama—on a

EATS FOR KIDS There are many cafés in the park, but the most popular is the **Pavilion Tea House** (Great Cross Ave., tel. 020/8858–9695), by the Royal Observatory. Sit at outdoor tables and order breakfast (all day), burgers, or baked potatoes with toppings. The park is perfect for a picnic on a fine day; buy picnic fare in Greenwich village from **M&S Simply Food** store (55–57 Greenwich Church St., tel. 020/7228–2545).

King William Walk, Greenwich, SE10.
Tube: Cutty Sark DLR or Greenwich DLR

 Free

🕐 Daily 6–6

☎ 020/8858–2608; www.royalparks.org.uk

🛒 All ages

clear day you can see St. Paul's Cathedral and the Docklands. No wonder, then, that at 155 feet above sea level, this site was chosen for the Royal Observatory (#16), also built by Christopher Wren. The observatory is home to the Prime Meridian line (longitude 00° 00° 00°), and the classic photo op where kids can stand with feet astride the point where east meets west. The hill is great for rolling, running, or sledding (when weather permits).

Having gone up the hill, you might return to the riverside or explore the boating lake or one of the tree-lined avenues leading to gardens. The Flower Garden by the lake is a riot of color, scents, and butterflies in summer. The Secret Garden Wildlife Centre has nature trails and bird-watching hides in the Wilderness, where you may spot the shy red deer that have bred here for centuries. For kids who'd rather climb and jump, a playground by Park Row Gate has enough apparatus to keep them happy for an hour or so. Check the park info boards for wildlife and horticultural activities.

KEEP IN MIND Getting here is part of the fun. Boats depart from Westminster Pier and pass the Tower of London during the scenic one-hour ride to Greenwich. By train, the elevated Docklands Light Rail (DLR) line runs through the ultramodern Docklands. If you get out at the Island Gardens station, you can walk to Greenwich underneath the river. Opened in 1902 to replace a 300-year-old ferry, the Greenwich foot tunnel is found near the *Cutty Sark* (#55). At its maximum depth, it is 53 feet beneath the river, and the pedestrian tunnel is just under ¼-mile long. It echoes eerily, or cheerily when filled with little voices.

MAKING THE MOST OF YOUR TIME At Elizabeth's Oak, the queen took tea in a hollow tree almost 6 feet across, which later became a tiny prison for people who broke park rules. You can also find what might be the remains of a Roman temple at the far end of Lovers' Walk.

HAMPSTEAD HEATH

Covering almost 800 acres, with beautiful hilltop views of London, Hampstead Heath (first mentioned in AD 986) is an ancient expanse of hilly parks, meadows, heath, woodlands, ponds, and lakes flanked by the historic north London villages of Hampstead and Highgate with their Georgian terraced houses. Today everyone comes to relax or to walk, jog, picnic, swim, fish, fly kites, rollerblade, or cycle. In earlier times, the heath was a wild spot, and washerwomen would use the ponds and hang the clothes of the wealthy on the prickly yellow gorse bushes.

The south end of the heath is the most appealing for kids because of its playgrounds and pool. You can get here easily from the station, beyond Nassington Road. Head to the Information Centre for a free map, and while you choose a route (guided walks are available), kids can explore the heath's history and wildlife through an interactive exhibit. An outdoor pool (admission charged) is beside the center; a free wading pool for smaller kids is between the jungle-style adventure play area and a more traditional playground.

KEEP IN MIND

Parliament Hill got its name because it was from here that Guy Fawkes and a co-conspirator Robert Catesby, who tried to blow up the Parliament in 1605, hoped to view their handiwork. Now, the foiled Gunpowder Plot is celebrated with fireworks every November 5.

EATS FOR KIDS **Parliament Hill Café** (tel. 020/7485–6606) at the foot of Parliament Hill dishes up Italian specials, plus salad, toasties, and cakes. You'll find kids' haddock and chips (for £5) at the old haunt of dandy 18th-century highwayman Dick Turpin, at **The Spaniards Inn** (Spaniards Rd., tel. 020/8731–8406). Or check the stag's heads at **The Bull & Last** (168 Highgate Rd., tel. 020/7267–3641) gastro-pub for popular £8 "baby" Sunday roasts, with beef and roast potatoes, carrots, and bobby beans. Pork belly roasts come with crackling, black pudding, and applesauce.

South End Rd., Hampstead, NW3. Silverlink rail: Hampstead Heath, from Highbury and Islington. Bus: 24, 46, 168, C11

 020/7332–3322; www.cityoflondon. gov.uk

 Free

 Heath daily 24 hrs

All ages

To walk on the wilder/higher side, set off east to the highest point of the heath, Parliament Hill. On weekends it's topped with colorful flying kites and always offers panoramic views of London way below. A walk northward takes you to the famous ponds, noisy with moorhens, coots, and model boats, and behind hedges are segregated swimming ponds for women and men. The ponds make a refreshing experience—if you don't mind sharing the water with waterfowl and creepy-crawlies. In summer, the coed pond below the East Heath is popular, but there's a small charge. In spring and late summer, the southern part of the heath hosts regular funfairs.

Beyond the tame attractions, you can discover the heath's natural beauty on trails ranging from 2 to 6 miles. Through woodland, wetland, scrub, and grassland, you can spot many bird species; bat walks are sometimes scheduled at night. Stay *alert*! During your return journey on a dusky summer evening, you might glimpse a fox, rabbit, or deer.

MAKING THE MOST OF YOUR TIME The

suggested route covers a small section of the heath, skirting East Heath and Parliament Hill, north and east of Hampstead village, although even this could take a meandering three hours. To see another beautiful part of the heath (little legs permitting), near Highgate, visit the area around historic Kenwood House (#42).

HAMPTON COURT PALACE

A long with wives, Henry VIII collected palaces, and Hampton Court Palace, sitting beside the Thames in acres of parkland, was perhaps the most magnificent. At the entrance to the cobbled Base Court at this picturesque Tudor-turreted royal palace, you can eavesdrop as a corpulent Henry VIII and his third wife-to-be Jane Seymour discuss their true love and the latest court intrigue. Lean in as actors in fine silk and royal regalia stalk the majestic palace, gardens, and English Baroque apartments and spontaneously break into historical tableau, playing famous Hampton Court habitués like the pleasure-loving Charles II as he prepares for a portrait with his favorite mistress, Lady Castlemaine.

This vast palace holds 500 years of royal history. It also holds 241 decorated chimneys and more than 5,000 objects on display, including 44 tapestries and 26 grand-scale wall paintings. Imagine the feasts and masques in Tudor times as you make your way through the hammer-beamed Great Hall dining hall. Then imagine all the work and food required to fuel such revelry as you walk through Henry VIII's kitchens, which were designed to

EATS FOR KIDS Choose between the **Tiltyard Café,** set among scented gardens and featuring a large menu of hot and cold food and kids' lunch boxes, and the smaller **Privy Kitchen,** which was originally Elizabeth I's private kitchen. On weekends, the Schools' Lunchroom in the Barrack block is available as an indoor picnic area, and inside the palace, visitors may picnic on the seats in the courtyards. Alternatively, bring a rug and picnic on the grass in the Tiltyard and Wilderness gardens.

East Molesey, Surrey.
Rail: Hampton Court

0844/482-7777;
www.hrp.org.uk

 £16.95 ages 16 and up, £8.50
children 5–15; £43.50 family tickets
(2 adults and up to 6 children aged
5–15); maze £3.85 ages 16 and up,
£2.75 children 5–15; grounds free

  Mar–Oct, daily 10–6; Oct–Mar, daily 10–
4:30; formal gardens daily 10–7 summer,
10–5:30 all other times; informal gardens
summer daily 7–8; daily 7–6 all other times

5 and up

feed more than 600 people twice a day. The Tudor kitchens are some of the most engrossing areas for all ages, and the castle provides an excellent quiz sheet to guide kids through the experience. In the hanging room you can peer in to see the game—swan, peacock, and boar; in the Great Kitchen you can see rooms packed with meat pies or a huge Tudor roasting fire in its full glory. Other Palace highlights include See William III's Withdrawing Room and Queen Mary II's crimson damask Audience Chamber.

Sightings of ghosts are legion, particularly "The lady in grey" in the southwest corner of the Base Court, and the ghost of Henry VIII's fifth—and executed—wife, Catherine Howard has been seen and heard rushing up and down the spooky Haunted Gallery. Allow adequate time to explore the 60 acres of gardens and get lost in the famous Hampton Court Maze, a maze commissioned around 1700 by William III and known for its confounding twists and turns.

KEEP IN MIND

Taking a boat from Richmond is the most panoramic way to arrive, but plan accordingly; the trip takes nearly two hours. Allow at least four hours at the palace to make the most of your visit.

MAKING THE MOST OF YOUR TIME Hampton
Court has a formidable series of free programs, including Tudor cooking events, Tudor dancing, medieval jousting, conservation of artifacts, and falcon displays. Ask at the Information Centre off Base Court, or phone ahead. If you're also planning to visit the Tower of London (#6), the Banqueting House, Kew Palace, or Kensington Palace, check out money-saving joint tickets for all four sights.

HMS *BELFAST*

Kids—big and small—love clambering on the big gun turrets of this Royal Navy light cruiser, Europe's largest preserved warship. Launched in 1938 and active during World War II and the Korean War, this docked museum provides a riveting way to explore wartime naval history and learn about life on board ship, from the quarterdeck to the Admiral's cabin. This big old ship saw plenty of action in its day and there's plenty to see here, from gun shells to ship's rations, plus videos and interactive games, so allow up to two hours.

The ship has nine decks and is divided into eight zones. The triple gun turret is a kid magnet. Lifelike models, flashing lights, vibrations, and frenetic voice recordings re-create what the crew of the *Belfast* encountered against the German battle cruiser *Scharnhorst* (one of the enemy's largest warships) during the epic Artic Convoys at the Battle of North Cape. The boiler and engine rooms down below are massive, necessary to drive this great warhorse, which, at full steam, ran at 80,000 horsepower. On other decks, you'll see the Ship's Company Galley, the Sick bay and Dental surgery, and learn about the hard life

MAKING THE MOST OF YOUR TIME The decks are linked by steep, ladderlike stairs, so wear comfortable, nonslip shoes. After your visit, stroll downriver across Tower Bridge for a view of the *Belfast*. The river path westward, the Millennium Mile, goes past the Millennium Bridge to the London Eye.

KEEP IN MIND Each of the HMS *Belfast*'s triple, 75-ton guns had a range of 14 miles. Currently the turrets are trained northward on the London Gateway service station on the M1 motorway. If you enjoyed this visit, you might want to check out more hands-on marine hardware in the Large Exhibits gallery at the Imperial War Museum (#44), where you can inspect a rare one-man *Biber* German WWII submarine.

Morgan's La., Tooley St., SE1.
Tube: London Bridge

 020/7940–6300;
www.iwm.org.uk

 £14 ages 17 and up.
Children 16 and under free

 Mar–Oct, daily 10–6; Nov–Feb, daily
10–5; last entry 1 hr before closing

 4 and up

of ordinary seamen, rum rations notwithstanding. (While serving for two years in Korea in the '50s, the crew washed down 56,000 pints of Navy rum.)

Augmenting the experience, videos show reenactments of the ship's heroic engagements, explain how important areas of the ship worked, and demonstrate what had to be done to make the ship watertight if a shell hit. On D-Day in June 1944, when the Allies landed on the Normandy beaches, HMS *Belfast* played a vital part in transporting and protecting the troops. Operation Neptune, the naval part of the landing—depicted in the opening sequence of the movie *Saving Private Ryan*—was a crucial turning point in the history of the war, and the *Belfast* remains to tell the tale. Check out the program of historical-themed workshops and free events to add to your visit.

EATS FOR KIDS The onboard **Walrus Café** is so called because of the tiny Walrus seaplanes that used to be stored here. Kids can admire the rivet- and pipe-lined walls while digging into a children's lunch box of sandwich, fruit, muffin, and drink (£5.50). A short walk away toward Waterloo Station, Gabriel's Wharf has a larger selection of eateries, including the **Gourmet Pizza Company** (tel. 020/7928–3188). The many wonderful pizza variations are big on creative toppings, and a boardwalk patio overlooks the Thames. See also the Tower of London (#6).

See the skeleton of an Irish giant, the cross-section of a famous brain, co-joined twins, and rare stillborn quintuplets floating—hauntingly—mouths agape, in glass specimen jars of 70% alcohol or formalin at London's quirkiest, possibly most weird, and definitely most potentially squeamish attraction at the awesome Hunterian Museum inside the august Royal College of Surgeon's HQ at Lincoln's Inn Fields. It's not for the faint-hearted . . . or the faint-stomached, either.

Here you'll find row upon row of well-lit glass cabinets full of skulls and skeletons, plus pickling jars of preserved brains, severed hands, feet, legs, bladders, grotesque tumors, and even the small-pox-ridden face of an unfortunate child from Lancashire—all beautifully displayed on illuminated glass shelves, like works of art.

Older kids with a curiosity for the bizarre and a penchant for body parts, CSI shows, and anatomy will adore this little-known gem of a collection, which showcases a selection from 3,500 anatomical, pathology, and zoological specimens and preserving jars amassed by the distinguished 18th-century Scottish surgeon and medical pioneer John Hunter

MAKING THE MOST OF YOUR TIME Between quizzes, trails, sketching materials, and a skeleton coat to wear and machines to hone your key-hole surgery skills, there's much to occupy older kids at Hunterian. Take your explorations a step further by dropping in on free basic suturing "Open Surgery" events led by medical students and professionals. At half-term and holidays you can meet the eccentric Jones the Bones skeleton for a journey around the human body, or hear about leeches, lancets, and bloodletting from a costumed 17th-century barber surgeon (booking essential). Forty-five-minute museum tours take place every Wednesday at 1 pm.

The Royal College of Surgeons, 35–43
Lincoln's Inn Fields, WC2A.
Tube: Holborn

 Free, £3 donation

 T–Sa 10–5

020/7869–6560; www.rcseng.ac.uk/
museums/hunterian

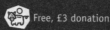 10 and up

FRS (1728–93). Body-snatcher, grave-robber, and friend of the "resurrection men," John Hunter pushed the boundaries of Georgian anatomy and scientific surgery as a top surgeon at St George's Hospital in London. His obsessive collecting streak didn't stop at humans: there are pickled giraffe eyelids from Africa, elephant intestines from the Queen's menagerie, kangaroo tongues, lizards, crocodiles, and random whale parts here, too.

As well as a set of early anatomical tables prepared for Great Fire of London-diarist John Evelyn in 1646, and surgical instruments belonging to Joseph Lister, one of the pioneers of antiseptic surgery, you can ogle and visually dissect the half brain of famous Victorian mathematician Charles Babbage (1791–1871)—considered a father of the computer—and the almost 8-foot skeleton of Charles Byrne, which Hunter may or may not have bribed undertakers to lay his hands on, and which he may or may not have boiled the flesh off to reveal Byrne's gigantic, awe-inspiring skeleton.

KEEP IN MIND John Hunter started out as an army surgeon in 1760 and spent three years in France and Portugal. He developed new ideas on treating gunshot wounds and venereal disease, and later moved to a large house in Leicester Square, which enabled him to take resident pupils and arrange his collection into a teaching museum.

EATS FOR KIDS Head out north across the atmospheric Lincoln's Inn Field (the largest public square in London) for the nearest best café, the **Fleet River Bakery** (71 Lincoln's Inn Field, tel. 020/7691–1457); sample healthy sandwiches, quiches, sausage rolls, and frittatas.

HYDE PARK

45

Spuddling around on a pedalo with the kids on the Serpentine in summer is a smashing way to sample one of the delights of Hyde Park, central London's largest green space, a famous Royal Park, and Henry VIII's former deer hunting ground. In fact, it is Henry VIII's Protestant reforming zeal we have to thank for today's 350-acre Hyde Park; he seized the land (known as the Manor of Hyde) from the monks at Westminster Abbey in 1536 following the Dissolution of the Monasteries so that visitors and locals alike could hunt here, too, albeit for recreation, not dinner.

If recreation is your family's game, you're spoiled for choice here. Take a horse or pony out for a one-hour group ride from the Hyde Park Stables (tel. 020/7723–2813, £64/hour, with hat and boots included) on the beautiful network of bridle paths. Take lessons and hire rollerblades from Citiskate (tel. 020/7193–5866), who meet at Queen Elizabeth Gate, or rent a boat and try to avoid other boats on the aforementioned Serpentine.

KEEP IN MIND
Now known as Rotten Row, and previously as *Route de Roi* (or King's Road), William III deterred brigands and highwaymen by lining the broad track running south along the park with 300 oil lamps in 1690 to link Kensington and St. James's Palaces, creating the first artificially lit highway in Britain.

EATS FOR KIDS The glass-fronted **Serpentine Bar & Kitchen** (tel. 020/7706–8114) commands a majestic position overlooking the Serpentine, and you'll find high-quality wood-fired pizzas, fish-and-chips, or fish finger butties with tartar sauce for around £6. Enjoy the lake-side terrace at the **Lido Café Bar** on the south of the Serpentine, where you'll find agreeable kids' hamburgers and chips, or mozzarella and tomato pizette for £4.60. Or under-6s dine for free for weekend brunch (12:30 pm–3:30 pm) at the **Cookbook Cafe** (1 Hamilton Pl., tel. 020/7318–8563) in the nearby InterContinental, off Park Lane.

Hyde Park, W2.
Tube: Lancaster Gate, Queensway, Marble Arch,
Knightsbridge, Hyde Park Corner

 Free

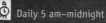 Daily 5 am–midnight

 www.royalparks.org.uk

All ages

In winter you can ice-skate at Hyde Park's Winter Wonderland, while the Joy of Life fountain alongside Park Lane is a popular spot to splash around and cool down in summer.

Other park highlights include the memorial to the victims of the 7/7 London terrorist bombings, the pet cemetery, and various sculptures—from a bronze long-billed ibis, to a colorful family of Jelly Babies. Public concerts have been a big feature since half a million fans turned up for the Rolling Stones in July 1969; these days the most rousing event is the relayed Proms in the Park in September, featuring the Union Jack–waving Last Night of the Proms from Albert Hall.

MAKING THE MOST OF YOUR TIME Soap-box ranters exercise their rights to free speech at Speakers' Corner near the Marble Arch section on Sunday afternoon, where anyone can step up and speak on any subject, so long as it's not profane or provoking violence. Heckling is *de rigeur*, and it is overwhelmingly good humored; you'll be following in the footsteps of Marx, Lenin, Engels, and George Orwell, who were frequent visitors here.

IMPERIAL WAR MUSEUM

The enormous guns flanking the entrance might suggest that this massive museum on the South Bank is merely a glorified showcase for war making, but it's far more than that. In addition to housing exhibits on 20th-century war tactics and machinery, it chronicles the human side of wartime—fear, bravery, and the spirit of camaraderie.

The impressive hardware on display includes howitzers, a Spitfire, Grant tank, Polaris missiles, a German one-man submarine, a Lancaster bomber, a V2 rocket, a Little Boy atomic bomb, and a bomber you can get inside. Among the numerous hands-on exhibits are the huge periscope that focuses on St. Paul's Cathedral and the Submarine section, where you can clamber inside and take the controls.

Other exhibits focus on life during wartime. Away from the front lines, the focus is on women's fashions and food rationing, while poetry and art reveal emotion in the heat of battle. The Blitz Experience gives a taste of London during the 76-night German air bombardment of World War II. In a reconstructed air-raid shelter on a 1940 street, you smell

MAKING THE MOST OF YOUR TIME Families should head for the theater past the ground-floor Main Entrance, where war-related films are screened at 10:30 am and 2 pm most days, including features on WWII aviation or old-fashioned Ministry of Information public information "food flash" short films on healthy war-time eating or surviving on rations. Interactive and object-led drop-in family events are held monthly, such as making a Remembrance Poppy Field, or sewing a "Make Do and Mend" wartime quilt.

Lambeth Rd., SE1.
Tube: Elephant and Castle, Lambeth North

 Free

Daily 10–6

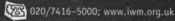 020/7416–5000; www.iwm.org.uk

6 and up

acrid smoke; hear sirens, fire-engine bells, and the bombs themselves; and imagine fearing your home has been destroyed. A reconstruction of a trench at the Somme in France in 1916, shows the ghastliness of World War I trench warfare. Lighting, sounds, and smells re-create what a "tommy" soldier endured, from trench foot (rot from constantly standing in mud and water) to the horror of climbing out of the trench into a barrage of gunfire.

The role of wartime secrets is touched on, too. On the ground floor you can decipher some Morse code, while on the first floor, an espionage and intelligence section has codebooks and invisible ink used by German spies in WWI, an original Enigma cipher machine, and a secret radio used by MI6 agents. Bringing the museum to life, Gallery Adventures are free kids' programs that run alongside special exhibitions (there are also events during school vacations). They include enactments of landmark events, such as the great POW escapes from Colditz castle. Prepare to battle over what to see first.

KEEP IN MIND
A testament to the millions of lives that were lost, the Holocaust Exhibition documents the persecution of Jews and other groups in World War II, giving personal stories behind the everyday objects, letters, and photographs. The exhibit can produce powerful emotions and might be distressing for children under 14.

EATS FOR KIDS Thankfully, the **Kitchen Front Café** is a ration-free zone. It serves freshly prepared hot and cold meals, kids' meals, and lunchboxes with a sandwich, fruit drink, cake, and fruit. Those who bring their own lunch can eat in a picnic room on the lower ground floor or outside in the gardens around the museum if the weather cooperates. Good supplies can be found at sandwich shops in nearby Kennington Road.

KENSINGTON GARDENS

Of all the London parks, Kensington Gardens is essentially the children's park, with its Peter Pan statue, wide open spaces, Round Pond boating lake, and Peter Pan–themed Diana, Princess of Wales' Memorial Playground. It was the princess who put Kensington Palace on the map, and along with inhabitants William III, Queen Victoria, and today her son William, and Kate (the Duchess of Cambridge), Diana was one of its most famous residents, situated on the eastern edge of the royal park.

Although Kensington Gardens seems to merge into Hyde Park, the Long Water, which leads into the Serpentine boating lake, separates the two parks. The asthmatic William III chose the fresh air and peaceful green fields of Kensington for his royal palace in 1689, and more than 300 years later, the park still has a rambling feel, far from the noise of Bayswater Road and Kensington Gore to the north and south. There are tranquil, formal gardens and fountains to explore in the elegant Italian Gardens—an ornamental water garden believed to have been a gift from Prince Albert to Queen Victoria. The Flower

KEEP IN MIND

The creator of Peter Pan, J.M. Barrie, lived a short walk away from Kensington Gardens at 100 Bayswater Rd. (look for the blue plaque on the house). It was on his walks through the park that he met the Llewellyn Davies boys, who were the inspiration for the Darling family and their adventures in Neverland.

EATS FOR KIDS

The chalet-style **Broadwalk Cafe & PlayCafe** (next to Princess Diana Memorial Playground, tel. 020/7034–0722) serves fun food to match the mood. Try a Serpentine and Elf sandwich (ham, cheese, bacon, chicken, and tomatoes) or flat-bread pizza. The **Orangery** (Broad Walk, tel. 020/3166–6112), with a beautiful setting next to the palace, is good for a kids' half-portion lunch or tea with cucumber sandwiches (£5.50); many young royals had their birthday parties here. The **Palace Café** (tel. 020/3166–6112) at Kensington Palace offers £4.95 Very Hungry Caterpillar lunch boxes, with cheese and ham sandwiches, hummus, yogurt, and raisins.

Bordered by Bayswater Rd., Long Water, Kensington Gore, Kensington Palace Gardens.
Tube: High Street Kensington, Lancaster Gate, Queensway

 Free

 0300/061-2000; www.royalparks.org.uk

Daily 6-4:15

All ages

Walk is a joy, with colorful displays year-round. Along the Long Water, a bronze Peter Pan statue is set in an enchanted woodland area, where kids can hide behind bushes. Peter plays his pipe to fairies, rabbits, and squirrels, which appear to pop out almost magically from the base of the statue. To the west is the Round Pond, where children sail toy boats amid gliding swans; if you're here at dusk, you may see bats flitting over the water.

The Diana, Princess of Wales' Memorial Playground, near the Queensway tube entrance, has sand, a huge wooden pirate ship, a music trail, and teepees. Children can swashbuckle on the galleon and hide in wigwams. Don't miss the ancient Elfin Oak by the playground. Sculpted in the bark of the hollowed stump, fairies, elves, and woodland animals look as if they could be charmed to life after dusk, when all visitors have left.

MAKING THE MOST OF YOUR TIME While you're here, a tour of **Kensington Palace** (tel. 0844/482-7777; www.hrp. org.uk) and a glimpse of the sumptuous lives of the seven princesses that lived here is a must. You'll find ornate gardens, a wiggly walk, and the grand state rooms and apartments at Prince William and Kate's formal London residence.

KENWOOD HOUSE

On the northern tip of Hampstead Heath, between the two charming old London villages of Hampstead and Highgate, lies the recently renovated Kenwood House stately home. The reasons to visit it are legion: you can tour (for free) the magnificent Robert Adam neoclassical mansion, along the way seeing some wonderful Old Masters paintings. Let the kids loose in the landscaped woodland gardens, and mount the high covered viewing stand just outside the grounds for a great view of the green space that survives so close to the city, and then continue your romp with a walk on the heath.

As befits a mansion transformed by Robert Adam in 1764 (originally built in 1616) for the Lord Chief Justice, Lord Mansfield, the house has sumptuous rooms. Of them, the Adam library is in a league of its own, with classic, curved ceiling decorations and columns that astound and amaze. Kids might prefer the paintings, however, including some of the world's most famous. *The Guitar Player,* by Vermeer; a Rembrandt late self-portrait; and *The Man with a Cane,* by Frans Hals, are included in a children's activity guide that

EATS FOR KIDS Kenwood's **Brewhouse Cafe** (note the Guinness connection), in the spacious white stable and coach house, is a family restaurant that, on weekends and during school vacations, serves kids' favorites such as macaroni and cheese, chicken, sausages, and salmon. Pastries and cakes make a scrumptious dessert. Walking to Hampstead, you'll find **Spaniards Inn** (Spaniards Rd., tel. 020/8731–8406), a historic tollgate pub with a pretty garden, paneled interior, log fires, and hot dishes of the day. Immortalized in Dickens' *The Pickwick Papers,* the notorious highwayman Dick Turpin, gentleman painter Sir Joshua Reynolds, and the poets Keats, Byron, and Percy Bysshe Shelley all drank here.

Hampstead La., NW3.
Tube: Archway or Golders Green, then bus 210

 Free

 020/8348–1286; www.english-heritage.org.uk

House daily 11:30–4; Gardens daily, 8–dusk (closing times vary with the season)

All ages

explains the house's history and highlights and prompts kids to write and draw their impressions and findings. Kids will also like the charming portraits of children, including one of the Duke of Wellington's goddaughter; *Miss Murray,* by Sir Thomas Lawrence; and Joseph Wright's exquisitely lit *Dressing the Kitten.* Tucked away upstairs is Lady Maufe's curious collection of 400 decorative shoe buckles—the sparkly ones would still be considered high fashion today.

Kenwood's gardens, its other great treasure, lead down to a lake with ducks and other waterbirds. In summer, this is the scene of outdoor evening concerts (from Blondie to Vivaldi), many of which end in spectacular firework displays. In spring, the rhododendrons and azaleas near the house are ablaze with color; this is a great place for playing hide-and-seek, as is the ivy tunnel. Another secret spot is the walled Kitchen Garden, where you can jump from step to step on the sundial while telling the time.

MAKING THE MOST OF YOUR TIME Kids may enjoy the restored Dairy at Kenwood House. They can enter the Buttery area to watch demonstrations of butter being churned by costumed staff—and help stir and pour the urns.

KEEP IN MIND Irishman Edward Guinness, the first Earl of Iveagh, bought Kenwood to house his paintings in 1924, and in 1927 bequeathed the collection to the nation. (This generous earl also set up houses in the poorer parts of the city for struggling Londoners.) The Guinness family wealth came from the now well-known brewing business.

KEW BRIDGE STEAM MUSEUM

This fascinating little museum is known worldwide for its Victorian Cornish beam and rotative pumping station engines, housed in a former Victorian pumping station with a tall standpipe tower. Each weekend from Easter to October, the engines are cranked up by a team of enthusiasts (the five Cornish beams once a month), who are also happy to answer questions about how these humongous pieces of machinery pump out water.

This particular pumping station supplied west London for almost a century, and the steam hall once housed six boilers. Three-level walkways enable you to appreciate the beasts' full size, and the operating machines let you experience a slightly steamy atmosphere. Now imagine a time when all the boilers were fired up and a team of brawny men hand-shoveled coal. This is a good trip for any kid who likes to see how things work, but the brightly painted beams, pumps, pistons, and flywheels—living sculptures that sing, hiss, and sigh with steam—also appeal to kids who just like to look at cool stuff. The engines have romantic names and interesting stories. The 1867 Dancers End Twin

MAKING THE MOST OF YOUR TIME The trip here takes about 30 minutes by train and 40 by Tube and bus; if you spend an hour or two at the museum, why not make an afternoon of it and picnic at the beautiful Royal Botanic Gardens at Kew (#19), about 10 minutes away back over Kew Bridge.

EATS FOR KIDS Open only on weekends 11–3:30, the **Café,** in the old boiler room serves lunchtime food that is far from old or boiled. You might find baked salmon, chicken curry, or vegetarian bakes, plus a soup of the day and sandwiches, on the daily changing menu. Main meals begin at £7, and smaller kids' portions are available. On weekdays, bring a picnic and eat in the steam hall or by the waterwheel outside if the weather is fine.

Green Dragon La., Brentford. Rail: Kew Bridge via Waterloo. Tube: Gunnersbury, then bus 237 or 267; Kew Bridge rail

 M–F £10 adults, £4 ages 5–15

 Tu–Su 11–4, open bank holiday Mondays

020/8568–4757; www.kbsm.org

 7 and up

Beam used to pump water to Lord Rothschild's country estate. One of the Cornish beam engines that once pumped here, the 1846 Grand Junction 90-incher, (described as "a monster" by Charles Dickens), is the largest 32-ton working engine of its type in the world. At full tilt it pumped 7.5 million gallons day, at 9½ strokes per minute.

The Water for Life gallery is a little more hands-on. It shows how the water system in London has worked since Roman times, including how it was used to battle against cholera, a serious water-transmitted disease. You can walk through a cross section of the present-day Thames Water Ring Main and explore life Down Below and a mock sewer tunnel.

Kids who like narrow gauge steam locomotives (think Thomas the Tank Engine) should visit the two beauties in the engine shed. Even better, come on Sunday from April to October when short rides are offered, so kids can let off some steam of their own.

KEEP IN MIND In addition to regular railroad weekends at the Kew Steam Museum (when you can ride on the locomotive Cloister), there are a host of special event weekends, including a live model-railway show, a festival of steam, and a historic fire-engine rally. The standpipe tower opens occasionally for intrepid stair climbers; on London Open House Weekend in late September, admission is free to this landmarked building.

LEGOLAND

LEGO lovers and Duplo devotees have a ball at this 150-acre theme park in Windsor that combines creativity and fun. The famous little Danish building bricks become larger than life in beautiful creations, and kids can build to their heart's content or enjoy more than 55 rides and attractions geared to a range of ages, from Atlantis submarine rides (with real sharks) to a brand-new Duplo Valley with dinosaurs, princesses, and clowns, to a new 1.5-million-brick Star Wars mini-land, which includes scenes from all six of the famous movies. The hardest decision is how to fit everything in, so study the map of the 12 play zones as the Hill Train descends into the heart of the park.

The top rides are in the farthest points of the park, where getting wet is part of the fun. You can whiz through the water on themed jet-ski pods in Adventure Land's Squid Surfer; take a quiet boat ride (with an ending that makes a big splash) in Pirate Falls Dynamite Drench in Pirates Landing; or survive a downhill dinghy chute in the Extreme Team Challenge in Duplo Land. Dry rides include the soaring Dragon, a coaster that twists and turns

MAKING THE MOST OF YOUR TIME Travel time to Windsor from central London is about an hour. Summer, particularly during school vacation, is the busiest time here, so if you visit then, come early to avoid lines for the top rides. Handheld Q-BOT devices (£15–£40) help you make the most of your time by allowing you to reserve a place in a virtual line for popular rides.

Windsor Park, Berkshire. Rail: Windsor, then Legoland shuttle bus. Bus: Green Line bus from Victoria Station

0871/2222-001; www.legoland.co.uk

£45.60 ages 16 and up, £34.20 children 3–15; online, adults £34.20, children £27.45

Mar–Nov, opening and closing times vary. Check online

3 and up

through the castle in Knights' Kingdom; the low-scream beginners' version is the Dragon's Apprentice. You can find rides on a gentler scale in Traffic Zone with Boating School and Drivers School, which let you navigate along routes. For high rides with cool park views, choose from Space Tower, Hill Train, Spinning Spider, and others. Little LEGO lovers can climb and explore in Duplo Playtown and then catch a breath watching Hans Christian Andersen's fairy tales take life in Duplo Theatre.

End the day with a stroll through Miniland, where 40 million LEGO bricks have been used to re-create world-famous sights. London's Tower Bridge opens to let boats through; in Paris, dancers do the cancan outside the Moulin Rouge; Scotland's Loch Ness Monster lurks beneath the water; and a rocket prepares for liftoff at Cape Canaveral. The list of instant entertainment options is long, even without the Imagination Theatre, where budding little builders get tips from pro model makers while older LEGO lovers design and build robots.

KEEP IN MIND

Entry is expensive, with one-day walk-up prices for 3–15-year-olds at £35.40. But book online and seven days in advance, and it's a more reasonable £26.55 per child. Summer is also the time when the most attractions are open. Check online for special events, such as fireworks evenings, stunt shows, and other seasonal performances.

EATS FOR KIDS There's something here to suit all tastes, including a Picnic Grove if you've brought your own treats. In LEGO style, City Walk **Pizza & Pasta** lets you construct your favorite flavor combination, or keep it simple with traditional fish-and-chips. For fresh grilled burgers, head to the **Crossed Ribs BBQ,** near Pirate Falls. Or kids eat free with a paying adult after 3 pm at the Knight's Table Rotisserie, Duplo Family Restaurant, and the Original Sandwich Co.

LONDON BRASS RUBBING CENTRE

39

Bordering Trafalgar Square since 1222, St. Martin-in-the-Fields is one of London's most charismatic churches, appealing even to kids. Known as the royal parish church, as many baby monarchs, including the infant Charles II in 1630, were christened within, the church is also known for its concerts, café, bookshop, and brass rubbing center. Yes, down in the crypt is the London Brass Rubbing Centre, where you can rub a brass to create a color image of a knight in armor, a gracious lady, a grizzly mythological beast, or an intricate Celtic pattern. The center's monumental brasses are replicas of some of England's and Europe's most important engraved memorial plaques. Copies are used in order to preserve the originals, which were walked on and rubbed by enthusiasts for centuries.

Plaques date to as early as the 11th century (notice the distinctly Norman names, such as the noble-sounding Sir John D'Abernoun, from Surrey) when they provided an eternal saintly image to which the living could pray. They also produced less clutter in churches than tombs and stone statues, and were cheaper, too. You can choose from about a

MAKING THE MOST OF YOUR TIME Free lunchtime concerts of classical music are given at the church by young artists every Monday, Tuesday, and Friday, as is a regular (admission charged) evening program, featuring groups like the London Oriana Choir. Note, the crypt gets really busy after weekend concerts.

EATS FOR KIDS To Londoners in the know, the **Café in the Crypt** (tel. 020/7766–1158) is celebrated for its no-nonsense, budget-price menu, which changes daily. There are usually hot meat and fish dishes (£6.50–£9.50) and a vegetarian option with homey English puddings or desserts (around £4). All profits go back to the church, which sponsors a charity for the homeless.

St. Martin-in-the-Fields, Trafalgar Sq., WC2.
Tube: Charing Cross, Leicester Sq.

 Free; image making
£4.50–£15

M–W 10–6; Th–Sa 10–8;
Su 11:30–5

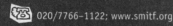 020/7766–1122; www.smitf.org

7 and up

hundred images, including such famous kings and queens as Henry VIII, Charles I, and Elizabeth I; elaborately festooned ladies; St. George and the Dragon; unicorns; Zodiac woodcuts; and William Shakespeare. Notice how fashion and armor—that is, chain mail graduates to plate armor—change over time.

Staff equip you with black or white paper, and show you how to make an outline and the first gentle rub with special metallic wax crayons, and how to correct blips. It's easy once you get the hang of it, and captivating. Allow 30–40 minutes to make a neat job. While kids are busy, adults can explore the church upstairs (designed by James Gibbs in 1726, a protégé of Sir Christopher Wren) or rub as well. And not to worry, the shop sells artists' images of the brasses if your own efforts disappoint.

KEEP IN MIND After you've completed your brass rubbing, see if you can read some of the worn tombstones on the floor of the crypt. Although people are no longer buried here, there are some famous tombs, such as those of Nell Gwyn from 1687 (Charles II's mistress) and Jack Sheppard, a notorious thief who was hanged at Tyburn in 1724. A tomb by the concert information desk has a wonderful skull and crossbones.

LONDON DUNGEON

Blood, bones, torture, murder, plague, and gore galore—what could be more appealing? The London Dungeon is the ultimate chamber of horrors, chronicling murderous and blood-curdling episodes from over 10 centuries of London's history. You might think that children will be squeamish—and some little ones are—yet strangely enough there are always hordes of kids eager to be scared out of their wits, making for long lines to get in, particularly on weekends and during the holiday season.

When you enter, scarily lifelike wax models show how grim it could be to live in medieval England. You'll find out what happens if you stole a piece of bread to feed your kids (you could be hanged) or spoke against the king (you could lose your tongue with the help of one of the torture instruments on display). If you didn't rot in prison with the (resident) rats, you might catch the plague, a revolting fate, as demonstrated by a poor victim showing postulated signs of the dreaded disease.

EATS FOR KIDS You'll find the friendly **Brazilian Las Iguanas** (tel. 020/7620–1328) five minutes along the Thames, next to the front of the South Bank Centre at the Royal Festival Hall. A £5.90 kids' meal can include chicken tacos, cheese quesadillas, fish strips or lamb meatballs, a drink, chocolatey cake, and vanilla ice cream. Or bank on £5.95 kids' salmon fillets, hot dogs, or grilled chicken breasts at **Giraffe** (tel. 020/7928–2004), just behind the Royal Festival Hall.

28–34 Tooley St., SE1.
Tube: London Bridge

 020/7403-7221; www.
thedungeons.com

 £24 ages 16 and up, £18.60
children 15 and under;
online £16 ages 16 and up,
£10 15 and under

Opening times vary;
phone or check online

 10 and up

But this is merely the mild beginning of your 90-minute tour, where costumed actor-guides take you from one historical horror show to another. In the Court Room, you may feel like an innocent bystander, but that doesn't mean you will escape courtroom punishment. You might be sent on a fast Boat Ride to Hell, via the Traitors' Gate. Amid tolling bells, howls, and screams, further journeys are linked by dark, catacomb-like passages lined with gruesome exhibits. In Jack the Ripper's London you'll witness tales of his terrible murders, after which he disemboweled his female victims. Watch out for the demon barber Sweeney Todd; Bloody Mary: the Killer Queen; and try to survive the Great Fire of London in 1666 by running the gauntlet of flames—well, not actually, but the pyrotechnics are pretty convincing. If you do survive, you can take home a gory souvenir from the gift shop. Severed arm, anyone?

MAKING THE MOST OF YOUR TIME You can buy cheaper tickets in advance online, or joint packages with the London Eye (#37) and Madame Tussauds (#33). Note: some exhibits, rides, and other parts of the tour are not advisable for people with nervous dispositions, pregnant women, or young children. Unaccompanied children under 15 are not admitted.

KEEP IN MIND London, like the rest of England and Europe, suffered from the Black Death, or bubonic plague, intermittently over 300 years. The first outbreak occurred in 1348. In 1665, the year of another major outbreak, diarist Samuel Pepys recorded that 6,000 Londoners died in one month. The disease, spread by flea-ridden rats, started with a rash, then fever, and swellings that turned black. Death would usually follow in two days.

LONDON EYE

For an unrivaled bird's-eye view of London, climb aboard the world's tallest cantilevered observation wheel. One of the most iconic additions to the London skyline on the buzzy South Bank, the 443-foot-tall, Ferris-like wheel takes you on a gentle 30-minute "flight" or (*very*) slow spin, with stupendous views over the city that, on a clear day, can extend to 25 miles away.

The flight appeals to young and old alike, and though from a distance the Eye looks a little scary, don't worry. Each of the 32 glass observation pods or capsules holds 28 people and are so spacious and comfortable and travel so slowly that you shouldn't feel motion sickness or claustrophobia. In fact, the Eye doesn't stop, even as you embark, except for visitors in wheelchairs. Inside, you can stand, walk around, take pics, or sit on the central bench and view London from a new perspective.

To the west, Big Ben's a stone's throw across the Thames, along with the Houses of

MAKING THE MOST OF YOUR TIME The lines can be long at peak times, but you shouldn't have to wait more than 30 minutes. Tickets are sold on a timed, set day, or seven-day flexible basis. Phone or online Fast Track tickets can be picked up in person 15 minutes before departure from County Hall, opposite the Eye.

KEEP IN MIND Although the London Eye looks like a Ferris wheel (named after the 19th-century U.S. engineer GWG Ferris), it's much more than that. Ferris wheels are supported on *both* sides of the wheel, but the Eye, spectacularly overhanging the river, is supported by a single A frame on just one side and by two 60-meter cables from concrete bases in Jubilee Gardens. Offering unobstructed 360-degree views, capsules are fixed to the outside of the wheel and are individually motorized so that no part of the structure restricts your view.

County Hall, SE1.
Tube: Waterloo, Westminster

 £17.01 ages 16 and up,
£9.96 children 4–15

Daily 10–8:30

0871/781–3000;
www.londoneye.com

 3 and up

Parliament, Westminster Abbey, and what most kids call James Bond's HQ: MI6, the government's secret service. Beyond are Nelson's Column and Buckingham Palace. To the east, you can see Somerset House, OXO Tower, Tate Modern, St. Paul's Cathedral, the Gherkin, the Shard, the Old Bailey law courts, HMS *Belfast,* Canary Wharf, and the O2 Arena. The Archbishop's Lambeth Palace is south of the Eye; the green spaces of Hampstead Heath, Muswell Hill and the spire of Highgate's village church lie to the north. Other highlights include the radio mast of Crystal Palace and Windsor Castle. You can survey the curvy Thames and its many bridges, the colored rooftops, and the city's usually private squares and courtyards.

If you are looking for unique viewing options, take a magical nighttime flight or one at Christmas, or at dusk. You can also combine your experience with a river cruise, enjoy champagne as you look out over London, or book a private capsule. The Afternoon Tea Capsule includes a traditional afternoon tea served during the flight.

EATS FOR KIDS Wander along the South Bank promenade a few minutes for torpedo rolls and minute steak at kid-friendly **Giraffe** (Riverside, Royal Festival Hall, tel. 020/7928–2004). Otherwise **Canteen** (Royal Festival Hall, tel. 0845/686–1122) has extensive kids' half portions at half price, including macaroni and cheese, chicken pie, or smoked bacon, pineapple, egg, and chips. Also walk farther along to Gabriel's Wharf and its restaurants.

LONDON TRANSPORT MUSEUM

*D*ing! *Ding!* All aboard! Tickets *PPPLEASSEE!!* What's not to like at the vintage bus and train-*tastic* London Transport Museum in the heart of Covent Garden, which tells London's gripping and ground-breaking transport history, from man-powered single sedan chairs and Thames-side wherry rowing boats, through trams, trolleybuses, horse-drawn omnibuses, steam trains, Metro-land electric trains, Routemaster buses, and black taxis.

Set in the picturesque 1871 iron-and-glass-roofed former Covent Garden flower market, kids will have a blast climbing, inspecting, fiddling about, and getting behind the wheel and pretending to drive many of the fascinating collection of 30-odd vintage trains, trams, Tube carriages, and London buses. Operate the "dead man's handle" on a 1930s Underground train; size up the Austin Low Loader first motorized taxi (originally from 1903); or George Shillibeer's 1829 first hail-and-ride London horse-drawn "Omnibus," which could carry 22 people on its original Paddington to the Bank of England service.

Shortly after 1 pm on January 9, 1863, the inaugural train of the world's first underground railway—known as the Metropolitan Railway—pulled out of Paddington station to be-

MAKING THE MOST OF YOUR TIME It's the details that make this such an enthralling museum. Check out the vintage leather strap handles or Underground tickets from 1924. There's an original 1933 London Transport map, the moquette shield design fabric used on '30s Tube train seats, plus bus hub caps, radiator badges, company rule books, ink stands, engravings, and a cool collection of iconic London Transport posters.

Covent Garden Piazza, WC2.
Tube: Covent Garden

 £13:50 over 16; under 16 free

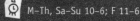 M–Th, Sa–Su 10–6; F 11–6

 020/7379-6344;
www.ltmuseum.co.uk

3 and up

gin a 3½–mile journey under the capital's streets toward Euston and King's Cross mainline stations, and into the history books—described at the time as *"the most stupendous engineering undertaking yet achieved in the railway world."* Here you can hear about the restoration of some of the first steam trains on the Metropolitan Railway—such as the E-Class 0-4-4T steam Locomotive No. 1—and inspect a same-series and archetypal-looking steam Locomotive No.23, built in 1866.

In the Tickets Please section you can play with Gibson ticket machines and toy ticket punches, and inspect old-fashioned seven-block wooden ticket racks; under-6s will enjoy the hands-on All Aboard section, where they can climb aboard or bump around as a passenger on minibuses, trains, Tubes, and taxis. Other fun activities include Track It Trails, storytelling sessions, and make-and-take arts and craft workshops where kids can make a classic red Routemaster bus or design a groovy Underground poster.

KEEP IN MIND In 1900, virtually every vehicle on the streets of London was horse-drawn. More than 300,000 horses were needed to keep the city on the move, hauling everything from private carriages to trams, cabs, buses, and delivery vans. But by 1915, everything had changed. Horse trams and buses had disappeared and motor taxis outnumbered horse-drawn cabs. Motor buses and electric trams were everywhere—Londoner's bus and tram journeys doubled, and in public transport the electric motor and petrol engine was king.

EATS FOR KIDS

Enjoy cool views over Covent Garden piazza **Upper Deck café** on the museum's first floor, where you'll find burgers and chips, fish fingers, sausage sandwiches, or kids' lunchboxes from £2.95 to £5. The **Lower Deck café** opens weekends and school holidays, and has ham, jam, or cheese sandwiches.

LONDON WETLAND CENTRE

You don't have to hike into the midlands to encounter curlews and plovers, goldeneyes, bitterns, pochard, teal, and widgeons—some of the fascinating waterfowl at a unique 105-acre site about a half hour from the heart of the capital. The Wildfowl & Wetlands Trust has creatively transformed four abandoned Victorian reservoirs in Barnes into a haven for freshwater-loving flora and fauna from around the world, and a fascinating, beautiful place.

Your visit begins in the Visitor Centre, where a film demonstrates that although wetlands are diminishing, they hold the key to earth's survival. This theme is expanded on in the Discovery Centre, with its models and games full of fascinating facts. Highlighting the whole experience is the spectacular two-story observatory, designed as a "bird airport" viewing lounge. Using a powerful telescope, you can zoom in on new arrivals—many fowl are migratory visitors—or watch waterfowl diving or digging for food, or sunning their feathers.

KEEP IN MIND

Although as much as 70% of our planet consists of water, barely 3% is freshwater. Wetlands are places where land and water meet, such as ponds, lakes, rivers, and swamps. Just about every plant and animal group needs a place of refuge in them.

MAKING THE MOST OF YOUR TIME
Even if your trip has "nice weather for ducks" (an English phrase for a rainy day), there's plenty to do here. The Discovery Centre has games galore with a learning angle. Kids can try on different animal heads and find out what it's really like to get a bird's-eye (or fish's-eye) view of the world. The Pond Zone is under cover, as is the observatory, and you can also make a dash along the paths and watch the ducks from one of the hides. Go Wildlife Watching with an Expert (£45/hr), or try a lecture or workshop like an Introduction to Birdwatching for over-11s.

Queen Elizabeth's Walk, Barnes, SW13.
Tube: Hammersmith, then free Duck Bus.
Rail: Barnes, then Bus 33 or 72

 £9.99 ages 17 and up;
£5.55 children 4–16;
£27.82 family

 Late Mar–late Oct, daily 9:30–6;
late Oct–late Mar, daily 9:30–5; last
admission 1 hr before closing

020/8409–4400;
www.wwt.org.uk

4 and up

Pathways radiate from the observatory and Discovery Centre to a series of zones that leap from the Tropics to the Arctic via chirrups, quacks, and squawks from geese and ducks of many gorgeous colors. Storyboards along the way make it easier to identify different species and learn more about them. Continuing on, you can walk on the Wild Side with its meandering pools and dense reed beds. Here, damsel and hawker dragonflies dance above you and Asian otters, water voles and shy amphibians lie quietly around—except for the lusty marsh frog, whose croak can be heard up to 650 feet away. Serious observers will head for the Peacock Tower, with its views over the main lake and Sheltered Lagoon; young visitors will enjoy the Pond Zone, watching mini-beasts under magnifying glasses, operating a pond cam, and using a net to dip into the water for creatures like smooth frogs or water scorpions, or making feathered friends with tame gadwall ducks. With six hides (shelters to observe wildlife), spectacular wild flowers, and 200 species of bird spotted over the years, the center is a place for young and old, at any time, as each season has its unique treasures—and the conservation values learned are priceless.

EATS FOR KIDS Shell and pebble decorations and water-themed food add whimsy to the **Water's Edge Café.** There are hot and cold buffet dishes, such as kid-friendly fish fingers. An outdoor terrace stays open until late in summer. Or amble along highly strollable Barnes High Street and try **Georgina's** (tel. 020/8166–5559) neighborhood joint for kids meals like spaghetti margharita, free-range chicken burgers, or ham, eggs, and chips for £6–£7.

LONDON ZOO

No longer places to merely stop and stare, modern zoos now spread the buzz on conservation and nature education, and London Zoo is no exception. Activities go far beyond watching and meeting some of the zoo's 16,800 animals, and it's unlikely you'll cover everything in one visit.

Naturally, the big beasts are a must-see. Sometimes you need patience to get a good look, however, because some of the larger enclosures have obscuring foliage and private areas to let the endangered species take part in the captive breeding programs. The family of the magnificent Sumatran tiger Raika is one of these success stories. At the Gorilla Kingdom you can meet the African western lowland gorillas Kesho, Effie, Zaire, and Jookie and watch them snack on coconuts, or mingling with colobus monkeys.

The Penguin Beach is a kid-magnet at feeding time (2:30–2:45). Bird enthusiasts will enjoy a stroll through the African Bird Safari, where rare exotic breeds fly overhead. Walk

EATS FOR KIDS The **Oasis Café** serves good-size portions of hot and cold meals as well as snacks. The **Animal Adventure Cafe** has sandwiches, salads, and packaged snacks to eat at the outdoor tables, and there are many grassy areas in which to sit and enjoy ices and milk shakes from kiosks around the zoo. Bear in mind that whatever you buy (including items at the well-stocked gift shop) supports the zoo's worldwide conservation work.

Regent's Park (Outer Circle), NW1.
Tube: Camden Town, then Bus 274

0844/7722-3333;
www.zsl.org/zsl-london-zoo

 June–Sept, £23 ages 16 and
up, £17 children 3–15, £65
family (2 adults, 2 kids);
Nov–Feb, £20 ages 16 and
up, £15.50 children 3–15,
£54 family

Sept 3–Oct 27, daily 10–5:30; Oct
28–Feb 15, daily 10–4; Feb 15–June
30, daily 10–5, July 1–Sept 3 10–6;
last admission 1 hr before closing

2 and up

through the re-created Rainforest Life to meet armadillos and rats, bats and slender lorises. In the Meet the Monkey's section you'll spot cute Bolivian black-capped squirrel monkeys, while the Reptile House (think black mambas, king cobras, and poison dart frogs) is a must for Harry Potter fans, as that's where Harry first spoke the snake-hissing "Parseltongue."

At the Animal Adventure children's zoo the petting of goats, sheep, donkeys, KuneKune pigs, and llamas is encouraged. But to meet the most important beasts on the planet, you *must* visit BUGS! In this huge glass pavilion, you'll discover—hands-on style—the importance of biodiversity, the delicate balance between humans, animals, and insects. Kids can see plenty of minibeasts up close, like leaf cutter ants and orb spiders, and question the keepers. If you have time, visit the breeding section, which has a good selection of tropical partula snails. Otherwise, kids can get creative in the art workshop and play area.

KEEP IN MIND

Kids won't want to miss the entertaining noontime Animals in Action display, where hawks, owls, parrots, and vultures swoop centimeters over head for strategically placed food and tidbits. The regular talks and encounters on spiders, megabugs, penguins, and giraffes are always a hit with kids, too.

MAKING THE MOST OF YOUR TIME Consider these

two ways to plan your day: You can follow the green footprint trail, which follows a circular route past the major exhibits; the trail can take all day in and of itself. Or you can shuttle between feeding times and animal-encounter sessions, noted on the Daily Planner sheet (available at the entrance). You may want to strike a balance between the two, as time and energy dictate. Whatever you do, come early to make the most of your time.

MADAME TUSSAUDS

The collection of waxwork models of the famous (and infamous) hardly needs an introduction, but the life of Madame Tussaud herself is less well known. The young Marie Grosholz learned her wax sculpture skills from a Swiss physician, who introduced her to French high society and she later became Louis XVI's sister's art tutor. During the French Revolution, she was captured and had her hair shaved for the guillotine but somehow managed to keep her head, along with her collection of wax death masks of guillotined nobles. The death masks were held up as revolutionary flags and paraded through the streets of Paris. Marie fled to England, where these gruesome models became a touring exhibition; settling first in Baker St. from 1835 and installed at their current location since 1884. Her first wax figure was of Voltaire in 1777 and she went on to make 400 models, from Robespierre to Benjamin Franklin.

KEEP IN MIND

The real human hair used on the models requires shampooing and grooming, but it isn't supposed to need a cut. Staff discovered that Adolf Hitler's hair appeared to be growing! Hitler doesn't get many hugs, but *Ab Fab*'s Joanna Lumley does; her jacket is often at the cleaners.

Your set route through 14 zones and 300 wax figures includes some of the original revolutionary heads and reveals how models are made. In the Sports Zone, kids can pose with champions like Beckham, Messi, Bolt, and Nadal. Premiere Night hosts stars of the big screen like Marilyn Monroe and Indiana Jones, while Culture Zone is home to great

MAKING THE MOST OF YOUR TIME
Come early so that you have time to enjoy all the waxworks. Prices vary according to the season, with full details on the website. Phone ahead for timed tickets that allow you to bypass the often lengthy lines, for an added £2 charge. Or book Late Saver tickets online for entry after 5 pm at a bargain £15 each.

Marylebone Rd., NW1.
Tube: Baker St.

 0870/400-3000;
www.madametussauds.com

 From £22.50 ages 16 and
up, £19.35 children 4-15;
family of 4 £81

 M-F 9:30-5:30, Sa-Su 9-6

 7 and up

minds like William Shakespeare, Einstein, and Charles Dickens. If you'd like an audience with the Queen—or the Duchess of Cambridge—you can find past and present royals in the Royal Appointment Zone.

The celebrity ranks have swelled in proportion to the public's appetite for the rich and famous. Socialize at an A-list Party, where you can sidle up to J-Lo, Nicole Kidman, or Brad Pitt and hear the latest gossip. As you enter the Music Zone to see Lady Gaga, Beyonce, Rihanna, and Justin Bieber you'll pass the paparazzi, trying to snap your pic.

The Spirit of London black cab ride takes you through 400 years of history (from the Great Fire of 1666 to the Swinging Sixties) and visits fun British characters like Benny Hill, but it's all a precursor to the final big thrill. In the Chamber of Horrors, torture victims and notorious killers—Dr Crippen, Vlad the Impaler, and Jack the Ripper—populate a world of scary sounds, scenery, and smells, with live actors dressed as psycho killers that jump out and stalk you.

EATS FOR KIDS **Caffe Nero** at Madame Tussaud's offers soups and panini. Popular chain **Pizza Express** (133 Baker St., tel. 020/7486-0888) is consistently good, with friendly staff in bright, Italian-style surroundings, although the pizzas aren't the biggest. Or stroll five minutes south to Marylebone High St. and stop for Belgium tartines, stuffed with tuna and hummus or prosciutto and mozzarella at long tables at **Le Pain Quotidien** (tel. 020/3657-6949).

MILLENNIUM BRIDGE

32

Not just any bridge, this 1,200-foot-long aluminum-and-steel span is the first new footbridge in central London in more than a century. (The Romans built the first bridge across the Thames, and the last was Tower Bridge in 1894.) While traffic buzzes across Blackfriars to the west and London Bridge to the east, you can discover the joys of strolling across the river without cars thundering along beside, and stop to admire the beautiful views. Designed by Sir Norman Foster—the architect of many iconic buildings on the London skyline and worldwide—and sculptor Anthony Caro, the suspension bridge connects the old (elegant, domed St. Paul's Cathedral) and the new (stark, red, oversize Tate Modern art museum) and stands smack in the middle of the Millennium Mile, a riverside walkway that takes in a clutch of popular sights on the South Bank.

The bridge opened in a blaze of publicity in 2000, and more than 90,000 people lined up to enjoy the so-called "blade of light" streaking across the Thames. The graceful, gleaming bridge does appear to fly effortlessly over the water, but its very lightness, plus

MAKING THE MOST OF YOUR TIME

After walking the bridge, why not walk the Millennium Mile on the South Bank? Actually, this much-visited section of the river contains two other walks: the Thames Path and the Jubilee Walk (with 1977 Silver Jubilee markers). Free maps are available at the City of London Information Centre. If you are interested in the area's history, discover more about the river and its bridges in an excellent display at the Museum of London in Docklands (#30). Those who like footbridges can explore Hungerford Bridge, which opened in 2003 and flanks the Charing Cross railroad bridge.

Bankside, SE1.
Tube: Southwark (south),
St. Paul's (north)

020/7332–1456 City of London
Information Centre, St. Paul's
Churchyard; www.cityoflondon.gov.uk

 Free

 Bridge daily 24 hrs. City
Information Centre M–Sa
9:30–5:30, Su 10–4

All ages

the overwhelming hordes on that first weekend, caused some swaying, ensuring a moving experience for all. Even though some swinging is expected with suspension bridges, the engineers closed it for modification. The bridge reopened in 2002, and today you'll find it a moving, yet unmoving, triumph. Although to this day, locals still refer to it as "The Wobbly" bridge.

The views are breathtaking, none more so than that of St. Paul's looming before you—the best river view of the cathedral and an artistic photo op. You can look downriver to the Tower of London, Tower Bridge, and beyond, and up to Somerset House, with the London Eye and Big Ben rising above the river bend. Down below, boats bustle back and forth. Don't forget to wave to people on the sightseeing boats. Afterward, stroll along Millennium Mile's red path to see how the other six bridges from Westminster to London Bridge compare.

KEEP IN MIND
Sir Christopher Wren, the architect of St. Paul's, might have given up if he'd encountered the same problems the builders of this bridge had to overcome. Work that was already behind schedule came to a sudden halt so that a rare breed of snail found on some old jetty legs could be rehoused, to the tune of more than £50,000. It just goes to show that small creatures can wield big power.

EATS FOR KIDS On the north side, grapple with a signature kiwi-burger at **Gourmet Burger Kitchen** (St Paul's Churchyard, tel. 020/7248–9199) with beetroot, egg, pineapple, and cheddar cheese, or sample three mini beef-burger sliders with American cheese, blue cheese, and onion ham for £10. Choose from 40 types of sweet and savory pancakes, or stick to sandwiches and cake at **House of Crêpes** (Gabriel's Wharf, tel. 020/7401–9816), on the Bankside.

MUSEUM OF LONDON

Before Buckingham Palace, before the Tower of London, grassland and ferns covered the land, and hairy beasts and flint-stone cave dwellers lived in what is now a modern metropolis. This engaging urban history museum shows the city's metamorphosis from 450,000 years ago, starting with the London Before London gallery. The regularly updated galleries display everything from 245,000-year-old wild ox skulls to Roman leather bikinis. Interactive displays and films help you discover more, but chatting with a guide in period costume or handling ancient objects is more fun, so find out about the day's scheduled events when you arrive.

You can walk through the museum chronologically, visiting a series of re-created sets such as a Roman living room and the 18th-century prison cell. The Victorian street with pub and shops is very Charles Dickens; the confectioner's shop has huge jars of traditional sweets that were sold by the ounce. You can also get a handle on everyday tools and objects, such as unusual weighing machines, and check out Tudor jewelry, which looks fashionable enough for today.

MAKING THE MOST OF YOUR TIME

Pick up activity sheets from the welcome desk, plus activity backpacks with Roman and Medieval London themes. Kids can meet a Roman Londoner, Charles Dickens, and Dr. Curiosity on Family Fundays, and check out the Museum's apps—on Roman Londinium and Dickens' London.

EATS FOR KIDS

The spacious **Entrance Hall Café** does a great job with soups, salads, and sandwiches; it's the best bet on weekends, when most eating places in the financial district shut down. Try a £5.30 Londoner sandwich, with bacon and Cumberland sausage. The **Sackler Hall Café** has inventive Wiltshire ham sandwiches, wraps, focaccia, and pesto pasta salads. The posher **London Wall Bar & Kitchen** (tel. 020/7600–7340) has £6 kids' mini cheeseburgers or scrambled eggs on toast for Sunday brunch 12–6.

150 London Wall, EC2.
Tube: Barbican, St. Paul's

020/7001-9844;
www.museumoflondon.org.uk

 Free

 Daily 10–6

 4 and up

Another approach is to head for the bigger galleries. The Medieval London gallery sheds light on city life in Londinium from the Roman to the Elizabethan age with many newly excavated objects—like marbles from the Temple of Mithras, and 1380s Poulaine pointy leather shoes. The War, Plague, and Fire gallery covers 1558 to 1666—don't miss Oliver Cromwell's death mask, a model of the Rose Theatre, and the film and diorama on the Great Fire of London, with flickering flames and diary extracts from Samuel Pepys. Marvel at the 1804 bird's-eye view of London from the middle of the Thames—the Rhinebeck Panorama—and explore the color-coded Charles Booth Poverty Maps, social history at its best.

Tradition is well represented with the glitzy coach used by the Lord Mayor for his centuries-old annual parade through the City. And there's plenty of hip and up-to-date stuff—a 1959 Vespa scooter; Biba, Mary Quant, and Alexander McQueen fashions; and a streetscape and photo-sculpture of a huge squat in London Fields.

KEEP IN MIND As the story goes, Dick Whittington came to London to seek his fortune, but when he didn't make money, he turned tail. As he was leaving, he looked back on the city, and the church bells, along with a black cat, told him to "turn again, Whittington." He did, and he became a great Lord Mayor four times over between 1397 and 1419. Don't confuse this mayor with the newer position of mayor of London. The traditional Lord Mayor is elected annually by the ancient livery companies of the City of London (the City isn't the whole city but one of London's oldest neighborhoods).

MUSEUM OF LONDON DOCKLANDS

The location of this museum about London's historic port, on a cobbled quayside beside water that reflects the gigantic modern tower of No. 1 Canada Square, brilliantly contrasts the old and the new at Canary Wharf. The journey is a mini-adventure in itself; it's a speedy ride from Bank station on the slick Docklands Light Railway, by Tube to the futuristic Canary Wharf station, or you can even arrive by boat. Then there's the romance of the building—an early Georgian warehouse for coffee, tea, sugar, rum, and West Indian imports—with original wood floor, beams, and pillars. Miraculously, it survived after the Luftwaffe rained bombs down in World War II. Resilience, as the museum makes clear, is the essence of the Docklands. The port that became the warehouse for the Empire and the world, stuffed with furs, feathers, and snakes, has seen trade go elsewhere. Today converted warehouse lofts have become a cool choice for London living.

You start on Floor 3 and wind your way along the fascinating, 2,000-year story of the port, which is told through films, push-button links, and engaging displays. Roaming visitor assistants provide further explanation and interesting anecdotes. The port of London

EATS FOR KIDS The light and airy museum **Café** has coloring sheets and tap water on request, as well as Pirates boxes, with sandwiches, hummus and cucumber, plus jelly and raisins. Accessed also from the street, the museum's **Rum & Sugar** restaurant has under-12s menus, including lamb burgers or battered cod and chips and Welsh rarebit on toast or penne pasta. Canada Square at Canary Wharf has more cafés and supermarkets for picnic supplies.

West India Quay, Hertsmere Rd., E14.
Tube: Canary Wharf. DLR: West India Quay

020/7001-9844;
www.museumoflondon.org.uk

 Free

Daily 10–6

 4 and up

was an exciting place, busy with trade and people coming and going. Bridges were crucial; check out the scale model of London Bridge as it was in the 15th century. Walk through 18th-century buildings that have been brilliantly re-created so that you can examine the scales and other port equipment, and peer into candlelit rooms and offices.

Sailortown is dark, dingy, and seedy, with its gas-lit warren of winding streets, a walk-in pub, shops, ale houses, and lodging rooms: it's perfect for contraband and dubious goings-on. If kids need reminding that crime doesn't pay, check out the ever popular 18th-century gibbet cage, used to hang the corpses of executed pirates. The Mudlarks children's gallery allows kids to let off steam; kids can sniff and guess smells, weigh and load cargoes, construct Canary Wharf, and get wet delving for "antiquities," among other hands-on activities. All in all, there's plenty here to keep kids captivated for an afternoon.

MAKE THE MOST OF YOUR TIME

A short section of the signposted Thames Path (www.national-trails.co.uk) makes a fun riverside walk. To the east are Island Gardens and a fantastic vista of the Queen's House and the Royal Naval College in Greenwich. A walk west takes you to Tower Bridge, past wharfs and famous Wapping pubs.

KEEP IN MIND Pirates were the scourge of the Thames, so punishment for piracy was gruesome. The gibbet cage on display in the museum would suspend a specially tarred dead body within it; the tar prevented the body from disintegrating too quickly in the water. There was even a notorious female pirate, Mary Read, who disguised herself as a man but came to a grim end, dying in prison from a fever. At Wapping Old Stairs, by the romantically named Waterside Gardens, pirates were hanged, then tied to a stake at the foot of the steps, where the tide would wash over them.

NATIONAL ARMY MUSEUM

More compact than the Imperial War Museum (#44), this place tells the British Army soldier's story from the country's first professional army—the Yeomen of the Guard—to the sophisticated British land forces of today, through paintings, photographs, uniforms, models, dioramas, and equipment. A tour of the gallery begins with the Redcoats, from Henry V and the crucial Battle of Agincourt in France in 1415 (the Brits won) to the army of George III, which fought in the American colonies (the Brits lost). Other battles depicted (with 70,000 model soldiers) include the Duke of Wellington versus Napoleon at Waterloo; don't miss the skeleton of Napoleon's favorite horse, Marengo, and the saw used to amputate the Earl of Uxbridge's leg, sans anesthetic—ouch!

Captivating battlefield models show the strategies employed, while life-size uniformed models are faithfully executed. Looking at them close up is interesting enough, but you can also try on some pieces, such as a heavy, uncomfortable helmet from the English Civil War (in which the Republican Roundheads fought the dashingly dressed Royalist

KEEP IN MIND

The souvenir shop here is a great place for fanatics of all things military, both national and international. You'll find model soldiers and a good range of books on military subjects. Plane-crazy kids should visit the Royal Air Force Museum, Hendon, London (tel. 020/8205–2266).

MAKING THE MOST OF YOUR TIME The interactive Kid's Zone play area eschews hand grenades and tommy guns, instead featuring forest and artic-themed climbing nets, rocking horses, and khaki uniforms to try on. There's also a hollow tree, a castle, slides, and other bouncy bits, plus coloring books and board games. In the hands-on Action Zone area you can find out if you're a drummer boy, infantryman, or cavalry officer, through a range of interactive games and quizzes. It's a popular attraction so slots are limited to 50-minute sessions.

Royal Hospital Rd., SW3.
Tube: Sloane Sq.

  Free

Daily 10–5:30

020/7881–6606; www.nam.ac.uk

6 and up

Cavaliers to defeat the monarchy from 1642 to 1646). In a display of arms and armor, you can lift a hefty cannonball and then imagine its destructive effects in battle. The modern army is covered through re-creations of a World War I trench and a WWII Vickers gun in Burma, as well as archival footage from both world wars, a piece of the Berlin Wall, and exhibits on the Gulf War and Afghanistan. An interactive computer section tests your military skills, from recognizing the uniforms and insignia of various regiments to surviving in a jungle expeditionary force. It's not all *Band of Brothers*, however, as the effects of war on civilians are presented, too.

In summer, costumed guides play historical roles, from archers in the Middle Ages to people doing vital jobs behind the front line, such as a female dispatch rider from World War II. You might meet up with one of Florence Nightingale's nurses; during the Crimean War in 1854, they pioneered the need for hygiene. In those days, more soldiers were likely to die from diseases picked up in hospitals than from wounds suffered in battle.

EATS FOR KIDS The museum's **Base Café** gives you a breather from attacking the museum's exhibits. Serving a range of snacks and good value meals using seasonal produce, it's also open to King's Road shoppers. For no-frills, cheap, and cheerful £6 meals like pasta or fajitas try **Stockpot** (273 King's Rd., tel. 020/7823–3175). Or slurp filling bowls of Vietnamese beef pho and rice noodles for £6.50 at the **Phat Phuc Noodle Bar** and courtyard, just off Kings Rd. (151 Sydney St., tel. 020/7351–3843).

NATIONAL GALLERY

More than 2,300 pictures by Western Europe's great masters are displayed in this magnificent—and unmissable—art collection, including some of the most famous works of art in the world. The museum's dignified, pillared building is part of London's celebrated Trafalgar Square, with its fountains, lions, and Nelson's Column. Today the square, known as "London's living room," is totally pedestrian-friendly and buzzing with visitors.

With such a vast wealth at your disposal, where to start? You could begin with the early Renaissance and Uccello's enthralling *The Battle of San Romano* fought between Florence and Siena in 1432, hung in the modern Sainsbury Wing. The West Wing has Titian, Cranach, and Hans Holbein, the artist who made it big by painting kings like Henry VIII. Then skip to the North Wing, for portraits and more by Dutch and Flemish masters like Vermeer, van Dyck, and Rembrandt, and move on to the East Wing for the Venice of Canaletto, the very British landscapes of Constable (think *The Hay Wain*), ships and sunsets by Turner, the France of Claude Monet, and works by Post-Impressionists van Gogh, Seurat, and

KEEP IN MIND Have a pencil ready for filling out the "paper-trails" booklets. Otherwise, you'll have to choose one from one of the gallery's shops, which also carry beautiful posters, drawing pads, and postcards. The trails are one of a packed program of daily events for families. Experts talk about a chosen painting from the gallery at lunch times, and shorter 10-minute talks keep youngster yawns at bay. Holiday art workshops for kids aged 5–11 are always popular.

Trafalgar Sq., WC2.
Tube: Charing Cross

 Free

 Daily 10–6, F 10–9

020/7747–2885;
www.nationalgallery.org.uk

 4 and up

Cézanne. Fine-tune your visit with ArtStart in the Sainsburg Wing, where you can tailor your own tour—great for older kids. Click on a readymade theme or create your own.

Another option is to join the free one-hour tours that depart daily at 11:30 and 2:30 or a family walk-and-talk session at 11:30 on Sunday. A carpet is unfurled in front of classic paintings like George Stubb's *Whistlejacket* equestrian portrait for magic carpet story-telling sessions on Sunday morning for under-5s (10:30 and 11:30). The Sainsbury Wing information desk has details. Self-guiding themed tour booklets, good for children 4–11, direct you to four corners of the gallery and invite kids to look, think, draw, or write poems, while fun audio guides (£3:50) include family trails like Teach Your Grown-Ups About Art, which turns the tables on adults and gets kids to lead you around.

MAKING THE MOST OF YOUR TIME It's best to enter the National Gallery from the Sainsbury Wing, to the west of the building, and not via the congested main entrance on Trafalgar Square. Here you'll find cloakrooms, a separate info desk, and an elevator that whisks you straight up to the second floor and the ArtStart area and main art collections.

EATS FOR KIDS **The National Café** (tel. 020/7747–5942) serves delicious lunches with international flavors, £6.50 kids' meals, and afternoon teas with cake and scones. Sit at long tables in the Bakery section of the upscale **National Dining Rooms** in the Sainsbury Wing for commanding views of Trafalgar Square (tel. 020/7747–2869). Try kids' macaroni and cheese or chicken and mushy peas for £6.75, or treat the kids to bargain English afternoon teas (£16.50), with finger sandwiches, scones, and jam.

NATIONAL MARITIME MUSEUM

A s citizens of an island nation, Britons have a deep reverence for the sea, and the world's largest maritime museum is the ideal place to dive into the nation's maritime heritage and its impact on the world. The neoclassical building and its location—in rolling parkland at Greenwich by the Thames, with panoramic views of London—are picture-perfect, and there's no better way to commence your maritime experience than to arrive by boat from Westminster or Tower Pier.

Humans inhabit just a small part of the planet, while the oceans are vast; potent reminders of this are the flashing lighthouse light and massive revolving propeller from a navy frigate that dominate the entrance. From the glass-covered Neptune courtyard with "streets" that highlight the past (in the shape of HMS *Implacable*, from the Battle of Trafalgar), present (shipbuilding and containers), and future (balancing trade and ecology), you can set sail to wherever your interest takes you. Computers and audiovisual installations grace the galleries, weaving imagery and facts in cinematic style.

EATS FOR KIDS
The nautically styled **Museum Café** has views of Greenwich Park and a changing menu of salad, fish, and vegetarian options, with kids' portions available on request. You can also find generously filled sandwiches and homemade bread at **Paul Bakery** on the upper deck of Neptune Court.

MAKING THE MOST OF YOUR TIME
Allow a day to discover all the treasures in Greenwich and leave some time and energy to explore the Royal Observatory (#16) and Palladian-style Queen's House (also free admission), both part of the National Maritime Museum buildings. The observatory is a short walk through the park, where you'll want to let kids run around and stand astride the famous prime meridian line of longitude.

Romney Rd., Greenwich, SE10.
Tube: Cutty Sark DLR

 Free

Daily 10–5

020/8858–4422; www.rmg.co.uk

7 and up

If seafaring adventures are your thing, indulge your fantasies in the Navigators and Voyagers galleries. From the swashbuckling privateer Sir Francis Drake to Captain Cook, who searched for passages to link the seas across the world, to the courageous Antarctic explorer Captain Scott, the history of exploration is covered comprehensively. Don't miss the star-exhibit navy-blue uniform that Lord Horatio Nelson wore when he was shot at the Battle of Trafalgar in 1805; you can see the blood stained breeches and the bullet-hole to the left shoulder. Likewise, Prince Frederick's 1732 royal barge—an intricately carved, 63-foot and 24-karat-gold-leaf royal pleasure poop (Shakespeare's phrase for a royal boat!), if ever you saw one.

In Nelson's day, children were part of a hard-working crew, and in the galleries on the second level kids can hoist flags, send a semaphore, steer a tanker on a rescue mission through Sydney Harbor, load a cargo vessel, and fire a cannon.

KEEP IN MIND Maritime doesn't just mean boats and navigation; it means having to do with the sea. The ocean is one of the world's great resources: 97% of the planet's water is stored in the oceans, of which we use around 1%. On your way out of the museum, look at the Environment gallery to see what you can do to save the oceans and waterways.

NATIONAL PORTRAIT GALLERY

The world's largest collection of portraits (1,000 in all), both painted and photographic, is presented in a cool setting, albeit in the shadow of its intimidating neighbor, the National Gallery (#28). A glass-encased escalator gives you a great bird's-eye view as you travel upward on a chronological ride in reverse, from modern times up—er, back—to the 1400s and the Tudor Galleries, a good place to begin. In those times, portraiture was the equivalent of political propaganda. Take Henry VIII: in Hans Holbein's portrait the powerful king is made to look more imposing and larger than life. The "Virgin Queen" Elizabeth I is immortalized with her white face and jewels.

Even though some early Old Master portraits appear a little stark to kids, the gallery presents them in a new light through crafty activities that inspire kids to trail through the gallery and copy portraits with colored pencils or fuzzy felt, match fabric swatches with designs they spot in the paintings, or act as a detective and spot hidden features in the portraits.

St. Martin's Pl., WC2.
Tube: Charing Cross, Leicester Sq.

 Free

Sa–W 10–6, Th–F 10–9

 020/7306–0055; www.npg.org.uk

7 and up

The Weldon Galleries showcase a wealth of talented characters from the Regency period. Among the great names in frames are Mary Shelley, who wrote her gothic novel, *Frankenstein* by the shore of Lake Geneva; Admiral Nelson, with his love, Lady Hamilton; Jane Austen, painted by her sister Cassandra; and monumental poets Lord Byron, William Wordsworth, John Keats, Percy Bysshe Shelley, and Samuel Coleridge. It's a brainy tour de force, but if period style isn't to your family's taste, zoom back down to famous faces from the 1950s to the 1990s, including Princess Diana, Sir Winston Churchill, Liz Taylor, and Jayne Mansfield, and artists like David Hockney, Francis Bacon and Andy Warhol, sometimes more famous than their subjects.

If traditional portraits don't appeal, focus on the changing photographic displays such as Mario Testino's gorgeous, glossy fashion mag pics of the Duke and Duchess of Cambridge, and contemporary retrospectives such as artist Man Ray's iconic Dada and Surrealist portraits and photograms. They're all free.

KEEP IN MIND
The original version of this famous Restoration London theater dated from 1663 (making it London's oldest theater site), but it burned down twice. Today's incarnation, completed in 1812, contains a huge auditorium that stages blockbuster musicals.

MAKING THE MOST OF YOUR TIME It's a good idea to call ahead for details about special free children's and family activities and tours (tel. 020/7306–0055) or check at the information desk as you enter. Ask for the free Making Portraits booklet, which asks questions and has space for drawing your own portrait, or try the drop-in family storytelling sessions or Family Art workshops.

NATIONAL THEATRE

Here's a chance for drama enthusiasts to get behind the scenes of Britain's most famous theater—to see how it all works and learn the tricks of the trade. You never know what might find—a great Shakespearian actor as you pass his or her dressing room door or a newfound passion for theater. At the very least, you will find yourself in awe at just how much of the stage magic happens out of the spotlight.

A guide with a deep knowledge of plays past, present, and future takes you into each of the three theaters—the Cottesloe, Lyttelton, and Olivier—that make up the 1963 National Theatre complex and explains the mechanics of each. Sitting in each one, perhaps catching part of a rehearsal, you discover how each one's shape and size are suited to specific types of plays and performances.

Backstage areas are like vast warehouses. You see entire sets ready to be wheeled in and out, just like freight on rail tracks. Countless props and furniture pieces—even glitzy

MAKING THE MOST OF YOUR TIME
Changing exhibitions of arts, crafts, and photography are presented in the large foyer area. Throughout the summer, the free Watch This Space program stages events on the open-air astro-turfed Theatre Square and kids' Playspace auditorium.

EATS FOR KIDS
The theater's **Olivier** and **Lyttelton Cafes** have the most family appeal—and are open based on performances. The **National Theatre Espresso Bar** has great coffee, pastries, baguettes, and outdoor tables. Watch out for the summer pop-up **Propshop** riverside café/bar, which is built from the theater's props—like a goose puppet from *War Horse* or light fittings (with severed limbs) from *Frankenstein*, and serves pulled pork sandwiches and lamb kebabs.

South Bank Centre, SE1.
Tube: Waterloo

020/7452-3400;
www.nationaltheatre.org.uk

Backstage tour £8.50
ages 18 and up, £7.50
under 18

M–F 4 times a day; Sat 2 times; Su
12:30 pm; tour times vary based on
performances

8 and up

chandeliers dangling high in the rafters—are recycled time and again. Not only can you peek at the props, but you can learn how they work and how they're made and hear fascinating tales about their stage successes and disasters. Kids will be interested to find out why there are eight understudy legs for the hand-sprung puppet horse Joey needed in *War Horse*, how the fake food for *Wind in the Willows* is made to look good enough to eat, as well as the secret to making real-looking blood spurt out at just the right moment . . . well, most of the time. In the scenery-making area, you see the genius of the carpenters and stage designers who turn planks and bits of foam or plaster into realistic-looking sets. Green-painted raffia becomes stage grass; hard sponge turns to stone; polystyrene becomes bombs.

At tour's end, follow a time line on the history of the theater, or head straight to the ticket booth to reserve seats for the next sizzling performance . . . so you can see all that backroom work from the front.

KEEP IN MIND Despite the National Theatre putting on 20 new productions a year (700 in total since opening in 1963), even the smartest stage props can go wrong. In one performance of *Peter Pan*, Smee, the pirate cook, had to improvise quickly when Captain Hook's hook suddenly shot out into the audience. He retrieved it. And in a grisly scene from *Macbeth*, a fake bloodied head was not made heavy enough. It ended up bouncing, like a ball, across the stage.

Huge neo-Gothic arches and spires with sculpted monkeys and animals merely hint at the natural history wonders to be discovered inside this Victorian treasure trove, home to more than 70 million artifacts. As you enter, a 105-foot *Diplodocus* skeleton known as Dippy—so large it dominates the Central Hall—greets you. From here, choose from the corridors leading off into the museum's vast acreage. Be selective—if you try to cover it all, you may become fossilized, too.

The Dinosaur gallery is the most popular exhibit for kids. A suspended walkway lets you look the stars of *Jurassic Park* practically in the eye. Pass *Triceratops* and *Stegosaurus* and at the end a ferocious-looking animatronic *Tyrannosaurus Rex* who roars, thrashes about, and fixes you with a hungry stare. Arthropods were around before dinosaurs, and they are introduced, in larger-than-life form, in Creepy Crawlies. Here you can walk through a 16-foot African termite mound or meet shell-sharing hermit crabs. In the Mammals gallery, you can walk the length of the largest creature ever—a life-size model of a 10-ton blue whale; while in the Birds section you can spot a flightless dodo from Mauritius—extinct

EATS FOR KIDS Kids with light appetites can refuel on baguettes and salads at the **Central Hall Café** by the main hall. Scoffasaurus kids' menus at **The Restaurant** in the Green Zone near Creepy Crawlies have more substantial crowd-pleasing mains like scampi or chicken burger with chips for £4.25. The **Deli Café**, by the Earth Shop, serves kids' toasted sandwiches, wraps, or tarts for £3.95, and has a healthy deli-style salad bar.

Cromwell Rd., SW7.
Tube: South Kensington

 Free

 Daily 10–5:50

 020/7942–5000; www.nhm.ac.uk

 4 and up

since the 1660s. Vivid glass marine models like the 1880s Blaschka jellyfish or single-celled radiolarian in the Treasures gallery are stunning works of art.

On your way to the Earth Galleries you can inspect objects that mark evolution itself: massive mollusk shells, whales' teeth, platinum nuggets and million-year-old rocks. Simulations demonstrate the earth's more spectacular movements, such as a video taken during the earthquake at Kobe, Japan, in which a supermarket floor shakes beneath you. Older kids like the Earth Lab, where they can check out fossils and precious rocks under microscopes, with the aid of museum scientists, to discover secrets of the earth.

The eight-story cocoon-like modern Darwin Centre—unsuitable for under-6s—hosts Archie the 8-meter giant squid and presents plants and creatures great and small (22 million in all) via touch-screen displays, films, specimen draws, and pickling jars and vats, from tiny frogs and butterflies to the giant Komodo dragon lizard.

KEEP IN MIND
At Investigate in the Green Zone, kids can experience what it's like to be a scientist, as they handle some of the museum's hoard of ancient bones, skin, teeth, meteorites, bugs, and more. Helpers show you how to weigh, measure, magnify, and discover more on computers about how these treasures fit into the circle of life.

MAKING THE MOST OF YOUR TIME Before you
get started, pay a £25 refundable deposit so kids can explore the museum with a fun Explorer Backpack, complete with explorer hats, binoculars, spotter cards, drawing materials, and trail cards. Also, free 30-minute Spirit Tours at the Darwin Centre of preserved zoological specimens are worthwhile and fun, too.

PALACE OF WESTMINSTER

Housing the famous green leather-seated House of Commons and red-seated House of Lords parliamentary chambers (as seen in those *feisty* debates on the BBC's Parliament Channel), plus ancient Westminster Hall, the Royal Gallery, and Elizabeth Tower and Great Clock of Westminster—Big Ben to us commoners—a tour of this historic, august, iconic, and soaring neo-Gothic pile and former royal residence beside the Thames is a must for its echoey corridors, stained-glass, statues, carvings, frescos, heraldic bosses, and the sense of Parliamentary history deeply interred here.

As you stand in the Venetian-mosaic tiled Central Lobby outside the Common's debating chamber, you can imagine brushing shoulders with members of the Cabinet, maybe the Chancellor of the Exchequer, a (*lost and confused?*) member of the Lords, or—*why not?*—even the Prime Minister.

The Norse king of England, Cnut the Great (995–1035), is believed to have built a residence here on the site of what was then known as Thorney Island, and successors like

KEEP IN MIND

After the calamitous fire of 1834, little of the original Palace of Westminster was left standing. Across the road, however, you can visit the remaining 1365 Jewel Tower, built for Edward III to house his jewels, and now with an exhibition on the history of Parliament.

MAKING THE MOST OF YOUR TIME

UK residents can arrange a free tour of Parliament through their MP or a member of the House of Lords. Or you can book tours on most Saturdays throughout the year and six days a week during the Summer Opening (July 27–September 1, Monday–Saturday) from Ticketmaster, or line up for unclaimed tickets on the day at nearby Old Palace Yard box office. You can line up for the (free) public gallery to watch debate in the House of Commons or House of Lords on Monday–Thursday, and on some "sitting" Fridays. Prime Minister's Question Time (Wednesday, from midday) can be spicy; check times.

St. Margaret's St., SW1.
Tube: Westminster

020/7219-3000 or 0844 847 1672;
www.parliament.uk

£15 adults,
£6 ages 5-15

Tours: Sa 9:15-4:30; Summer Opening
July 27-Sept 1, M-Sa 9:15-4:30

9 and up

Edward the Confessor (1005–66) established the predecessor of Parliament, the great *Curia Regis* (or "Royal council") in Westminster Hall, which met as a parliament in 1265 and later as a wider "Model Parliament" in 1295. Henry VIII switched his royal residence from here to the Palace of Whitehall in the 1530s but it remains officially a royal palace. Despite its royal status, a foiled 1605 Gunpowder Plot to blow it to smithereens, catastrophic fires (in 1834), and 14 hits during the Blitz, the Palace of Westminster has housed Parliament and various royal law courts ever since.

Taking in the hammer-beamed Westminster Hall—which has seen famous trials (Charles I, Guy Fawkes), coronation banquets (George IV), and lying-in-state (Sir Winston Churchill)—and following the Queen's route during the State Opening of Parliament, the 75-minute tour climaxes in the Common's Chamber where you can stand where the Prime Minister stands and spot the Speaker's Chair and red lines on the floor separating opposing political parties—*supposedly* two sword-lengths' apart.

EATS FOR KIDS You'll find soups, sandwiches, and Cornish pasties at the **Jubilee Café** off Westminster Hall. Opposite Big Ben, kids can listen out for the "Division Bell" (which rings to warn that there are two minutes to vote in Parliament) and try egg mayo sandwiches, fish-and-chips, or pork pies and Piccalilli relish, at the traditional pub **St Stephen's Tavern** (10 Bridge St., tel. 020/7925-2286), frequented by Prime Ministers, politicos, and advisors since 1873.

REGENT'S CANAL

From Little Venice to Camden, a beautiful stretch of the Regent's Canal is one of London's best-kept secrets and a magical slowboat trip for the entire family. Cutting through the leafy northern section of Regent's Park and at times almost invisible from the busy roads above, the early Victorian canal is its own tranquil world. Willows trail in the gently lapping water, waterbirds buzz about their business, and stately herons stand still as statues. Magnificent stucco houses with palatial private gardens sweep down to the water at Regent's Park, and the charming small gardens of Camden's tall Victorian houses come with their own bobbing rowboats.

The easiest way to explore is on a tour given by Jason's Trip canal boats, out of Little Venice. From the elegant John Nash stucco houses that overlook the canal and little basin (marina), it's easy to see how this oasis got its name. The tiny, tree-filled Browning's Island, named after the poet Robert Browning, who lived within sight, is lined with gaily painted houseboats, which also appear at other basins farther along the canal. The 100-year-old *Jason* narrow boat is similarly rigged out. Once inside, you can well imagine how compact you'd have to be to live in one.

MAKING THE MOST OF YOUR TIME Allow an afternoon
for your visit so that you can browse the stalls at your leisure and stop for food in Camden. The London Waterbus Company (tel. 020/7482–2660 recording) connects Camden Lock and Little Venice, stopping at London Zoo (zoo admission included in some tickets). Hourly service runs daily April–October, weekends November–March.

Jason's Trip, Blomfield Rd., W9.
Tube: Warwick Ave. Museum, 12–13
New Wharf Rd., N1. Tube: King's Cross

020/7286-3428; www.jasons.co.uk
or www.canalmuseum.org.uk

Single boat trips £8, £7
under 14; museum £4, £2
children 7–15, families £10
(2 adults, 3 kids)

Apr–Nov, daily 10:30, 12:30,
2:30, plus 4:30 Sa–Su June–Aug;
museum Tu–Su 10–4:30

All ages

A lively guide provides commentary along the 45-minute nonstop ride. One highlight for kids is passing through London Zoo (#34), where they can get a bird's-eye view of the Snowdon Aviary, see an antelope ambling about, and catch a whiff of the giraffe house. Among the historical anecdotes, you discover that the canal was a working route, where boats laden with coal were pulled along the towpath by horses. At a tunnel, the horses were unhitched and the boatmen had to "leg" through it. The men lay on their backs on planks aboard the boat and "walked" the boat, using the tunnel sides.

Above the towpath at Camden Lock and journey's end, a year-round marketplace teems with life. Craft shops and vintage fashion stalls are a mecca for shoppers. The loud music and bustle are in marked contrast to the gentle lull of life below the bridge.

EATS FOR KIDS

The Summerhouse (tel. 020/7286–6752) canal-side restaurant has great views of the canal and £6.50 kids' meals, like salmon fishcakes and crêpes and ice cream or knickerbocker glories. **The Red Pepper** (8 Formosa St., tel. 020/7266–2708) is a jolly pizzeria. Pizzas are large, so kids can share. Near Camden Lock are restaurants and take-out places galore.

KEEP IN MIND To enjoy the canal for free, walk the towpath, open dawn–dusk. The prettiest part is from Camden Lock to Prince Albert Bridge, where you can access Regent's Park. For a nontourist route, go east from Camden Lock to picturesque St. Pancras Lock, where you can take the bridge to Euston Road and St. Pancras Station, near the British Library.

REGENT'S PARK

Probably the most perfect of London's royal parks, 18th-century Regent's Park was designed by John Nash for the Prince Regent. The elegant terraces of grand, cream-stucco houses sweep the Outer Circle's perimeter and buffer this haven from noise. An Inner Circle connects many recreational areas, too, such as open spaces for playing, rose gardens, playgrounds, a boating lake, tennis courts, wildlife garden, sports fields, and an open-air theater.

Start from York Gate where York Bridge leads to the Inner Circle and the gilded gates to Queen Mary's gardens. In June, this stunning floral epicenter is breathtaking with the scents and colors of the magnificent rose garden's 30,000 roses (400 varieties in all). Traipse across the Japanese bridge to discover a cascade and duck island in a little lake. Look carefully, and you may see a posing heron. Also nearby are a waterfall and fountains with tiny pergola secret gardens. If you time it right, you can see a children's play at the open-air theater—open May to September. Shakespeare's *A Midsummer Night's Dream* never had a more perfect setting. The park comes alive with the sound of music with

KEEP IN MIND

Primrose Hill, to the north, on the far side of the Regent's Canal and Prince Albert Road, is part of Regent's Park. Climb up to its grassy hilltop (no more primroses, alas), and you'll be rewarded with a superb panorama of the park and the London skyline.

EATS FOR KIDS Cafés include the **Garden Café** in the Inner Circle, which has a large patio and offers soups, salads, and macaroni and cheese. The family-run **Boathouse Café** by the lake has pasta, chicken, and flat-bread pizzas, and **The Honest Sausage** on the Broadwalk near London Zoo specializes in free-range organic sausages and bacon, with a Park Porker in a soft bun with onion sauce and organic mustard for under £5. Alternatively, pick up gourmet snacks and sushi at **Pret a Manger** (120 Baker St., tel. 020/7923–5233) if arriving via Baker Street Tube.

Regent's Park, W1.
Tube: Baker St.,
Camden Town, Regent's Park

0300/061-2300, 0844/826-4242
theater; www.royalparks.gov.uk

Free

Daily 5–sunset

All ages

weekend and summer jams in the bandstands, and is overrun for the hip Frieze London art fair in October.

Outside the Inner Circle is a boating lake where you can rent a pedalo or rowboat for an hour and navigate a wildfowl island. For more action, kids can bounce around in one of four playgrounds. Maps are posted at most entrances, or get one from the Information Centre, at the east end of the Inner Circle.

Peer through the railings of London Zoo (#34), and see some of the animals for free. Camels, elephants, exotic birds, and an occasional lion are on the left side of the zoo and giraffes are opposite the entrance. For smaller wildlife, visit the wildlife garden or the leafy canalside (*see* Regent's Canal, #22), where barges ferry visitors from Camden Lock to Little Venice.

KEEP IN MIND As you walk across the beautifully landscaped lawns and among the formal flower beds, watch your step. During World War II, the park was used by the military, and no fewer than 300 bombs (including German V2 rockets) fell on the grounds. The once undulating land was flattened by infilling with dumped bomb rubble. Even today (though not often, so don't worry too much), the ground can cave in where the fill is loose and where there are pockets or old air-raid shelters.

Prepare to discover your inner fighter ace, and whether you've got the *right stuff*, at the former Hendon and London Aerodrome in Colindale (the cradle of British aviation), where over 100 glorious, intoxicating, and full-size war planes, helicopters, and vintage aircraft spectacularly chart the role of the Royal Air Force in the development of aviation in the UK since the turn of 19th century.

Kids will find some wonderfully cool aircrafts from the dawn of aviation, ranging from a Blériot XI single-prop monoplane (the first plane to fly the English Channel, flown by Louis Blériot in July 1909) to a single-seat 1916 Sopwith F1 Camel which saw service on the Western Front and became the highest scoring fighter in WWI.

In other spacious hangers—and often suspended dramatically in the air—you'll find incredible classics like a 1910 Clarke Glider, a Vickers Vimy bomber (1917), an Avro Rota autogyro spy plane (1934), a Hawker Hurricane (1937), a Spitfire I (1938), a Lancaster

KEEP IN MIND Hendon Aerodrome has been an important center for aviation since Henry Coxwell and James Glaisher were the first to fly from Hendon in a balloon called the Mammoth in 1862. The first powered flight from Hendon was an 88-foot nonrigid airship in 1909, built by Spencer Brothers and piloted by Henry Spencer (an Australian suffragette, Muriel Matters, was the only passenger). The first true flight was by French aviator Louis Paulhan, who flew 117 miles from Hendon to Lichfield on April 27, 1910, and then on to Burnage near Manchester the next day, easily the longest flight in the UK at the time.

Grahame Park Way, NW9.
Tube: Colindale

 Free

 020/8205-2266;
www.rafmuseum.org.uk

 Daily 10–6

 3 and up

bomber (1941), and a Messerschmitt Swallow (1942). Modern jets and aircrafts include the fuselage of a twin-engine Boeing Chinook transport helicopter, and a BAe Harrier GR3 jet fighter.

Black Hawk flight simulators in the Milestones of Flight Gallery or Historic Hangar, let you swoop, bank, shudder, and feel what it's like to grapple with a Bristol monoplane in a WWI dogfight over France; tear around in a Tornado jet on a low flying mission through the valleys; fly a Eurofighter Typhoon at *twice* the speed of sound; or man a Red 7 with the daredevil Red Arrows.

There are 40 hands-on exhibits and real or simulated cockpits to climb into at the Aeronauts gallery, where kids can learn how aircrafts fly, and test their vision and pilot reaction times. Finally, you can watch a moving 13-minute "Our Finest Hour" sound-and-light show on the hour 11–5 in the evocative Battle of Britain Hall.

MAKING THE MOST OF YOUR TIME Special events
are held on D–Day, Remembrance Day, and US Independence Day, and activities for children take place all year. Popular workshops can include activities like decorating a poppy collage for Remembrance Day, drawing exercises, Search and Rescue role play games, Pulsar Battlezone interactive laser games, and face painting. There's a 4-D Theatre (£4 each), which combines 3-D computer animation with dynamic seating where kids can go on a B17 bombing mission in enemy territory or navigate through ravines and canyons at supersonic speeds.

EATS FOR KIDS
Besides indoor and outdoor picnic areas, you can sit amid helicopters at the **Wessex Café** in the Historic Hangar for tea and light bites, or £1 cheese sandwiches. The **Wings Restaurant** (tel. 020/8358–4936) has more substantial fare, including "small person meals."

ROYAL BOTANIC GARDENS, KEW

Here, on 300 pretty, peaceful acres beside the Thames and Kew village, you can discover more than 30,000 species from the plant kingdom at this UNESCO World Heritage Site. The Victoria Gate visitor center has guided and self-guided Habitat Trails to get you tracking down plants and brushing up on your botany skills. Guides are on hand to answer questions, or download a free app from the website for some interactive fun with Kew's plants, sites and exhibits as you amble around (*zapping* plant labels as you go).

The gardens began in 1759 with the 9-acre botanic collection of Augusta, the Princess of Wales, on the grounds of Kew Palace. The collection grew, and wonderful garden buildings, such as the striking 10-story, red-gray brick Chinese Pagoda, were added. Other fabulous buildings followed. The huge Temperate House and Palm House conservatories, by Decimus Burton are inspiring. Elevated walkways let you climb up around the palms, and a marine section contains giant kelp, a plant used in lipstick and ice cream. Bananas grow in the Palm House, as do cocoa trees, giant bamboo, and the superclimber

KEEP IN MIND

Little kids can crawl and comb through the wild Jack in the Beanstalk world of the Climbers and Creepers play zone. In this great rainy–day distraction, kids will digest a few fun facts about gardens as they slide through the mouths of carnivorous plants or scramble through a bramble tangle.

MAKING THE MOST OF YOUR TIME
It's worth visiting the redbrick Kew Palace inside the gardens; it's a doll's house lookalike and the smallest surviving Royal palace. Built by Flemish merchant Samuel Fortrey in 1631 and known as the Dutch House because of its rounded gables, Queen Caroline leased it in 1729 as an annex to Richmond Lodge, and it became a nursery for the royal children, with George III spending much time here as a boy. Highlights include a cute baby house or doll's house, which is believed to have been made by George III's daughters.

Kew Rd., Kew.
Tube: Kew Gardens.
Rail: Kew Bridge

020/8332–5655; www.kew.org

 £16 ages
17 and up

Mar–Aug, M–F 9:30–6:30, Sa–Su and holidays
9:30–7:30; Sept–Oct and Feb–Mar, daily
9:30–6; Nov–Feb, daily 9:30–4:15

 All ages

Hairy Mary. Stop by the Evolution House and whiz through 40 millennia to study early fossils and see how plants have shaped our world. If exotic is your thing, walk across the world's climatic zones in the Princess of Wales Conservatory; here you see prickly cacti, giant water lilies to rival Monet's, a Venus flytrap, and plants that look like stones.

And that's just the indoor stuff. The 40 assorted buildings are mere dots on this ever-changing landscape of formal gardens, lakes, arboretums, and woodlands. Don't miss the Bamboo Garden with its bamboo musical instruments or the tall timber Treetop Walkway—an exciting way to see Kew from above. Your kids will get muddy scrambling through the Badger Sett, and there's a Stag Beetle Loggery to spot endangered sap-roxylic insects. Finally, try Treehouse Towers for zip wires and scramble nets, or survey Kew's giant compost heap—one of Europe's largest.

EATS FOR KIDS You can do a £4.70 pick-and-mix kids' lunch box at the **White Peaks Café** near Climbers and Creepers. Or enjoy kids' corn on the cob or pork and leek sausages with mash and gravy for £4.50 at the **Orangery** (tel. 020/8332–5953) restaurant near Elizabeth Gate. The **Original Maids of Honour** (tel. 020/8940–2752) on Kew Rd. is a quaint 120-year-old tea room, where you'll find chicken and ham pie or famous lemony Maids of Honour tarts (so beloved by Henry VIII that he confiscated the secret recipe and sealed it in an iron box in Richmond Palace).

THE ROYAL INSTITUTION

Test for poison, electrocute frogs, send SOS Morse code, or crush a glacier. These are just some of the irresistible things you can do at the museum of the venerable scientific society, the Royal Institution, in Mayfair. Established in 1799 by the leading British scientists of its day, to carry out research and popularize science. Famous chemists and physicists—such as Sir Humphry Davy, Michael Faraday, John Tyndall, James Dewar, Lord Rayleigh, and George Porter—carried out much of their major research and popular lectures here. (Davy famously tried out his new discovery of nitrous oxide—or laughing gas—at a public lecture here in 1801, to . . . *hilarious* effect.)

Luckily the frog-electrocution and glacier crushing are achieved virtually, when you use the RI's ingenious handheld eGuide device (£3 each), which plays witty interactive animations of historic scientific developments at regular intervals throughout the museum. These interactive guides are a cute way to get budding scientists, and technology lovers, zipping and zapping through the historic *and* state-of-the-art exhibits.

EATS FOR KIDS Share a BLT or club sandwich with chips at the museum's **Bar & Café** (tel. 020/7670–2956) for £8.25, or try cheddar cheese or bacon and brie toasties for £5, from 3 pm onward. Upscale **Napket** (tel. 020/7629–4622) on nearby Piccadilly offers pasta Bolognese for £5.64 and Parma ham and mozzarella sandwiches £5.95. Or treat kids to the soaring double-height elegance of **The Wolseley's** (tel. 020/7499–6996) grand all-day café/dining salon on Piccadilly, where you'll find fishcakes (£6.25), eggs Benedict (£7.25), or traditional cream teas with scones for £9.25.

Albemarle St., W1.
Tube: Green Park

 Free

 Mon–Fri 9–6

 020/7409-2992; www.rigb.org

5 and up

Some of the most important scientific discoveries have been made at this institution, like Davy's discovery of sodium and potassium, and Faraday's historic work on electric motors and electromagnetism. At the in-house Faraday Museum you can see the preserved 1850s laboratory where Faraday first harnessed electricity, discovered benzene, and carried out experiments liquefying gas and rewriting theories on electrochemistry. Directly opposite, in a neat juxtaposition, is a latter-day lab where white-coated scientists can sometimes be spotted working on special projects, such as making nano-magnets to neutralize cancer cells.

On the first Saturday of the month (except December and January) families can drop in for hands-on Family Fun-day activity sessions 11–4, like rocket building, boat making, or exploring waves (£10 adults, £5 over-3s). Book ahead for the Royal Institution's experiment-packed children's Christmas Lectures, which have enthralled kids since 1825; topics include everything from modern-day alchemy to how to convert a bicycle wheel into a gyroscope.

MAKING THE MOST OF YOUR TIME Royal Institution president Sir Humphry Davy (1778–1829) invented the Davy safety lamp in 1815 to combat deadly explosions in coal mines, caused by the buildup of methane. His use of wire gauze around the lamp's wick was a great success— a method still used to protect the Olympic flame.

KEEP IN MIND Michael Faraday (1791–1867) started out as an apprentice to the village blacksmith, and at 14 was apprenticed to a bookseller in London, where he read many books. At 20, he attended lectures by the eminent chemist Humphry Davy at the Royal Institution, and after he sent Davy a 300-page book based on what he learned at the lectures, he became Davy's assistant. Faraday's invention of the electric motor, transformer, and generator, ushered in modernity, and he became the first lifetime Fullerian Professor of Chemistry at the Royal Institution, and the *main* scientific advisor to the State and the Royal family.

THE ROYAL MEWS

The Queen's palace is London's stateliest sight, with guards standing sentry inside the ornate black-and-gold gates (*see* Changing the Guard, #63). But equally impressive are the gilded coaches and elegant black carriages that sweep out majestically along the Mall with their horses and liveried coachmen on state and royal occasions. These glorious coaches are kept in the stable courtyard, or mews, at the side of the palace and can be seen along with some tack and the horses themselves.

The first stage of your visit passes the Riding School, where the Cleveland Bay or Windsor Grey horses are trained. It's a rigorous program that includes pulling broad, heavy weights and learning to keep cool while bands play and crowds wave flags and shout. Queen Victoria's young family of nine was schooled in riding here, but not the current princes William and Harry.

Next come the carriages, stationed outside each numbered door. They are decked in highly polished leather, red-and-gilt paint, and shiny brass lanterns and are quite

KEEP IN MIND

If you were wondering what the word "mews" means, it is from the French word *mue*, which means to shed an outer coat, or moult. In days of old, the word was used for the place where hawks and falcons were kept when they were shedding their feathers.

MAKING THE MOST OF YOUR TIME
Families can take a free family audio tour, led by a young livery man. Kids will find out what it's like to drive a Rolls-Royce, train the Queen's horses, or ride a fairy-tale carriage through the crowds and streets of London on grand state occasions. At weekends and school holidays, youngsters can also dress up as Albert the Coachman or design a royal carriage in the Family Activity room.

Buckingham Palace Rd., SW1.
Tube: Victoria

 020/7766–7300;
www.royalcollection.org.uk

 £8.25 ages 17 and up,
£5.20 children 5–16,
£22 family

 Daily Apr–Oct 10–5; Nov–Dec 21
and Feb–Mar 10–4; last entry
45 mins before closing

4 and up

high off the ground. So how *does* the Queen ascend regally? A swift response comes from one of the stewards: a footman unfolds steps from inside the carriage door. George III's 1762 Gold State Coach is the must-see masterpiece, almost completely gold with cherubs and two mythical Tritons on the back. These stately vehicles don't race, but proceed at walking pace, pulled by four pairs of horses with postilion riders and accompanying footmen, all in red-and-gold regalia. The Queen used the coach for her 1952 Coronation, her 1977 Silver Jubilee, and her Golden Jubilee in 2002.

It's unlikely you'll catch the Queen in the stables, although she does name each horse herself. Her Majesty is an accomplished rider, and the beautiful little saddles used by the young princesses Elizabeth and Margaret are on exhibit in the Harness Room. One appears to be decorated with flowers; if you look close up, you'll see they are little shells sewn together.

EATS FOR KIDS Head toward Victoria Street rather than Buckingham Palace Road for a better selection of eateries, such as the slick and solid Asian noodle joint **Wagamama** (Cardinal Place, off Victoria St., tel. 020/7828–0561). Try mini yaki soba noodles with chicken, or cod cubes with sticky white rice for £4.15. The excellent **Spaghetti House** (3 Bressenden Pl., tel. 020/7395–0390) serves truly Italian pastas, pizza, and meat dishes in a friendly modern bistro setting. There's kids' spaghetti carbonara and Nutella pizza for £5.

It's about time you visited the observatory that keeps the world ticking *in* time. Synonymous with time and its connection with the earth and sea, the Royal Observatory Greenwich was established by Charles II in 1675 to find a solution to the problem of calculating longitude (those thin, vertical lines that you see on globes) at sea. Work by various astronomers and decades of dogged effort by clockmaker John Harrison (1693–1776) produced a solution in the 18th century. The 0° longitude line—the Prime Meridian—was established at Greenwich in 1884 by international agreement. Greenwich Mean Time is based on this. Pause in the observatory courtyard to see the meridian—shown as a brass line across the cobbles. A photo, legs astride the western and eastern hemispheres, is a must.

The museum traces the history of astronomy and the search for navigational longitude. It's an absorbing place for kids who love planets, seafaring, and timekeeping. There are telescopes, clocks, chronometers, and other exquisite historical timepieces as well as exhibits charting discoveries by such royal astronomers as John Flamsteed, after whom the

KEEP IN MIND The red ball on top of the observatory drops down the rod at 1 pm on the dot, just as it has every day since 1833. Sailors used this system to set their clocks precisely to Greenwich Mean Time. Before then, the sun and stars were used to measure latitude, but without an accurate onboard clock they couldn't determine their longitude. Without that knowledge, many a ship came to a disastrous end, unable to find its destination precisely or on schedule. Boats were shipwrecked and crews starved because sailors couldn't determine time and longitude accurately enough.

Blackheath Ave., SE10.
Tube: Cutty Sark DLR

020/8858-4422;
020/8312-6608 planetarium;
www.rmg.co.uk

Observatory free; Meridian
courtyard £2 ages 6–15, under 6
free, £10 annual pass includes 3
children; planetarium shows £6.50
ages 16 and up, £4.50 3–15

 Observatory daily 10–5; planetarium
shows weekends/holidays, 11–4:15,
weekdays 12:45–4:15

 7 and up

building (designed by Christopher Wren) is named, and Edmond Halley, of comet
fame. Among the treasures are the sea clocks, H-1 to H-5, that Harrison made to
measure longitude at sea.

You can touch a 4.5-billion-year-old meteorite in the astronomy galleries, plus
man the flight deck and send a virtual space probe to Venus. Nearby, look
through London's only public camera obscura: with a small aperture in the roof,
a mirror, a round table, and a completely dark room, it shows a 360-degree
image of the outside world, in this case a panorama of Greenwich Park (#50).
The Peter Harrison Planetarium has up to eight 25-minute star shows a day—
from Space Safaris for under-7s to shows on exploding stars and galaxies. On
scheduled dates you can peer through the huge refracting telescope to view
planets with the help of an astronomer. As you leave, don't forget to check
your watch by the grand old 24-hour clock still ticking away.

**MAKING THE
MOST OF YOUR
TIME** Greenwich makes a
great outing, especially if maritime and historical sights appeal.
Allow a day to see everything—
particularly if you come by boat
from Westminster or Tower Pier.
If the weather's fine, you'll want
to explore Greenwich Park and the
Royal Naval College (see #50), too.

EATS FOR KIDS If you don't want to go far, the **Pavilion Tea House**
(see Greenwich Park #50), opposite the observatory, is your best choice. Also nearby
is the National Maritime Museum (#27); you can eat in its restaurant. Another option is to browse around Greenwich center and see what you like. In fine weather,
buy picnic fixings and explore Greenwich Park to find a royal spot for your meal.

ROYAL OPERA HOUSE

Budding opera buffs and ballerinas will be belting arias from the rafters and spinning pirouettes in their sleep after an engrossing one-hour-15-minute backstage tour of the Royal Opera House in Covent Garden; it's a must-experience in one of the most famous and sumptuous opera houses in the world.

Housing the Royal Opera and the Royal Ballet, and hosting touring companies like La Scala and the Kirov, kids will get a tingle down their spines stepping off Bow Street or the piazza as they enter the beautiful, airy glass-ceilinged foyer in the heart of Covent Garden. Glamorous photos and busts of greats like Dame Margot Fonteyn, Maria Callas, and Rudolf Nureyev are reminders of some of the legendary dancers, divas, and performances that have graced Covent Garden's proscenium stage over the years—from *Swan Lake* to *Sleeping Beauty*.

Built in 1732, and initially called the Theatre Royal, it presented its first opera and oratorios under German-born Baroque composer George Frideric Handel in 1734, although it served primarily as a playhouse for its first hundred years. The backstage tour, led

KEEP IN MIND

After the theater was rebuilt in 1809, the actor-manager, John Philip Kemble, raised seat prices to recoup costs. The move was so unpopular audiences disrupted performances by beating sticks, hissing, booing, and dancing. The Old Price Riots lasted two months, before management caved in to their demands.

EATS FOR KIDS Boasting views over Covent Garden piazza, the grown-up **Amphitheatre Restaurant** (tel. 020/7212–9254) is open for non–theater ticket holders for lunch and afternoon tea, and has macaroni and cheese and orange jelly for £7 for non-grown-ups. The **Amphitheatre Bar** has a double round of smoked salmon sandwiches to share for £11.50. Or the **Paul Hamlyn Hall Balconies Restaurant** overlooks the spectacular old Covent Garden Flower Market floral hall, and has kids' meatballs and mash for £8.

 Bow St., W1.
Tube: Covent Garden

 020/7304-4000;
www.roh.org.uk

 Backstage tours £12, £8.50
children ages 8–15; tours M–Sa;
check online for times

 Daily 10–3:30

 8 and up

by passionate production staff, will fill you in on the theater's colorful history like the two times the theater burned down—in 1808 and 1857. You'll also learn about the time when the theater was requisitioned by the Ministry of Works as a furniture repository during WWI, and how it became a dance hall hosting tea dances during WWII.

You'll see stunning backdrops, fly bars, and gigantic stage sets, wagons, and stage turns, as well as touring the costume, props, wig, and jewelry departments, and look in on Royal Ballet rehearsals, where you might see a prima ballerina or the corps de ballet perfecting pirouettes.

Each tour is unique because the Royal Opera House puts on about 20 productions a year, but one thing's for sure: you'll be blown away by the grandeur of the magnificent 2,256-seat auditorium, with its four-tiered amphitheater, royal boxes, and balconies, and its plethora of gilt and plush red velvet seats.

MAKING THE MOST OF YOUR TIME If your
kids have never been to a live performance at the ROH before, you can apply for cheap £5–£20 special Welcome Performances of popular kid-focused ballets like *Swan Lake* or *Alice's Adventures in Wonderland*; kids can meet the ROH's creative team, fiddle with props, try on costumes, listen to readings, or play instruments from the resident orchestra. Apply online for these brilliant full-length performances (up to three hours), which occur two or three times a year.

SCIENCE MUSEUM

Eyes and minds are opened wide at this world-famous Science Museum in South Kensington. With a world-class collection of 300,000 scientific items, more than 20,000 of the best objects on display on seven floors and 12 galleries, and more than 800 genuinely fun, diverting, and often cutting-edge interactive experiences, figuring out where to begin is not an exact science. The trick is to either come early with bags of time and energy; be ruthless and highly selective about what you see and explore; or just wander about, allowing serendipity, not science, to guide you.

However you choose to explore, be sure to visit the futuristic and interactive Atmosphere gallery on climate change where you can explore climate science, CO_2 levels, and the challenges of global warming. Check out an Antarctic ice core, wave your hand to discover how the sun's energy travels the globe, and look at proposed solutions like a hydrogen-powered urban car.

EATS FOR KIDS The self-service **Energy Cafe** inside the Energy Hall has cakes and sandwiches, or head for something more substantial at the high-tech blue neon-lit **Deep Blue** restaurant on the ground floor; a £4.95 children's menu consists of scampi or cheeseburger and chips, sausage and mash, and mac-and-cheese, plus a drink and dessert. Fun LED screens display daily menus in the self-serve **Revolution Café**, and the **d. café** in the new Dana Centre has tuna melt or turkey breast New Yorker toasted ciabatta sandwiches for £5.95.

Exhibition Rd., SW7.
Tube: South Kensington

0870/870-4868;
www.sciencemuseum.org.uk

 Free; IMAX £10 adults, £8
children 5-16, family tickets
£27 (2 adults, 2 children);
charges for special exhibitions

 Daily 10-6

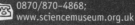 3 and up

Launchpad's 50 hands-on exhibits and experiments on physics and the forces of nature are always a big draw. With helpers on hand, kids can run a radio on pedal power, make a rainbow, or inspect their noses on a thermal imaging screen. Interactive gadgets in the Who Am I? gallery in the Wellcome Wing, allow kids to morph their faces to look older or younger, and find out where their ancestors lived. There's an IMAX cinema with 3-D shows on oceans and space stations, plus SimEx and Motionride simulators that send you flying down glaciers or scampering from dinosaurs.

Don't overlook the older world-altering exhibits, like the 1813 *Puffing Billy*—the oldest remaining steam locomotive—or George Stephenson's 1829 *Rocket*, the first locomotive engine to pull passengers. Look out for Alexander Graham Bell's first telephone, a replica of the *Apollo 10* Command Module, Charles Babbage's Difference Engine No. 2 (a forerunner of the modern computer), and Crick and Watson's double-helix DNA.

MAKING THE MOST OF YOUR TIME
There are free daily half-hour guided tours of the excellent Space, Flight, and Making the Modern World galleries, and 40-minute curatorial tours of English scientist James Watt's reassembled 1819 workshop, which exhibits 8,430 extant items from when he died. Ask staff for times of demonstrations and performances, and check online for monthly Science Night sleepovers (£45, for ages 7–13, accompanied by an adult).

KEEP IN MIND
Need an excuse to miss school? Check out the Who Am I? gallery, which explores some the strange genetic diseases. You could have a sudden case of didaskaleinophobia (a fear of attending school). Or how about decidophobia (a fear of making decisions)? And as for a dreaded visit to the doctor, well, there's always a sudden case of iatrophobia.

SHAKESPEARE'S GLOBE

On the South Bank, under bundles of water reeds and buttressed by English oak, William Shakespeare's artistic home has risen again. Shakespeare's Globe was the dream of the late American actor and film director Sam Wanamaker, who tried to find Shakespeare's London theater in 1949. All that was left of it then was a plaque on the wall of a brewery, but through his efforts the Globe was reborn in 1997, 750 feet from its original site and a few centuries after its 1600s heyday (the original burned down in 1613 when a cannon went off during a play!). Your admission to the Globe's exhibition includes a 40-minute tour of the theater, although during summer matinees this is replaced by a visit to the site of an earlier Elizabethan theater, the Rose.)

From the moment you step into the replica open-air theater, you enter a time warp. As guides explain, few concessions to modern technology were made in its construction. Everything was done by hand, without electricity, as in Shakespeare's day; there's not a nail in sight. Those water reeds make the only thatched roof in London, as such

KEEP IN MIND

Shakespeare's Globe is known as the wooden "O" after Shakespeare refers to it in *Henry V*; "*Can this cockpit hold the vasty fields of France? Or may we cram Within this wooden O the very casques that did affright the air at Agincourt?*"

EATS FOR KIDS Kids enjoy old-fashioned English eggy bread and baked beans with a drink or smoothie for £10 at the **Swan** (tel. 020/7928–9444) bar and restaurant at Shakerspeare's Globe, a classy joint with stunning views overlooking the Thames, Millennium Bridge, and St. Paul's Cathedral. For more dining ideas, see Borough Market, *Golden Hinde*, and Tate Modern.

21 New Globe Walk, Bankside, SE1.
Tube: London Bridge

 020/7902-1400;
www.shakespearesglobe.com

 Exhibition £13.50 ages 16 and up, £8 children 5–15, family £36 (2 adults, 3 kids); performances: groundlings £5, seats from £15 ages 16 and up; family £110 (2 adults, 2 kids)

 Exhibition open daily 10–5:30; theater season late Apr–Oct

8 and up

roofs were banned after the Great Fire in 1666. Oak forms the supports, seats, and stage, and performances use original methods, too, without microphones or spotlights. Music is provided by lutes, pipes, citterns, tabors, drums, and other instruments of the time—you can see them in the exhibition—and actors stroll from thrust stage to audience as the play demands. When cannon fire was needed for *Henry V*, the *Golden Hinde* replica, just along the riverbank, obliged.

Shakespeare's Globe exhibition celebrates the Bard's plays—from *Hamlet* and *Macbeth* to *King Lear*—and includes gorgeous costumes. Demonstrations of stage combat or costume making often take place in the exhibition. Drawings, paintings, and diary entries show that Southwark, with its playhouses, alehouses, and bull and bear baiting, was London's playground in the days of the original Globe. Today Southwark is enjoying a renaissance as one of the liveliest sections in town.

KEEP IN MIND If you want to experience the real thing—and perhaps be a groundling—attend one of several Saturday matinees during the summer season. Running concurrently with these is ChildsPlay, the ultimate in cultural babysitting. While parents enjoy a performance, children attend this workshop (£12.50), which zooms in on bite-size sections of the play and sparks imagination through drama, storytelling, and art. Kids then watch the last 20 minutes in the theater. If they're ready for a full play, check kids' discounts and note that schedules vary.

SOMERSET HOUSE

A former Royal palace—from James I to Catherine of Braganza—and one of London's architectural treasures, the neoclassical 18th-century, riverside Somerset House has squeezed out the dreary government offices that were once here and opened itself to the public. The front (Strand) entrance brings you to the Courtauld Gallery (#57), with its magnificent art collection; the back (Embankment) leads to the contemporary art Embankment Galleries. Between is an elegant courtyard reminiscent of an Italian palazzo, which hosts open-air ice-skating (November–January), concerts and films, art exhibitions, London Fashion Week shows, and a summertime grove of 55 water fountain jets for kids to splash around in.

The most exciting way to arrive is by foot from Waterloo Bridge. You can imagine how London was in the 18th century, when the river lapped Venetian-style at the building's water-gate entrance and Navy Board barges (the Royal Navy had offices here) arrived from Greenwich. You can see the Commissioners' Barge at the old river level, beneath the

KEEP IN MIND Admiral Nelson, an important figure on the Navy Board, reported regularly to Somerset House. Although his character looms large, he was actually "a thin, spare naval officer with only one arm. . . . His frail figure shook at every step."

The Strand, WC2.
Tube: Covent Garden,
Holborn, Waterloo

 020/7845–4600;
www.somersethouse.org.uk

 Free

Daily 10–6

 4 and up

Great Arch, bearing the face of Old Father Thames. Join the free 45-minute guided tours of Somerset House on Thursday and Saturday for tales of Tudor intrigue, like the Popish Plot, Georgian Enlightenment, and Civil War Puritanism—taking in the Seaman's Hall, the Deadhouse, and the Nelson Stair.

The Fountain Court is the hub of activity on many weekends, particularly in summer: kids can enjoy free music performances, mime, and more to watch, plus children's drop-in art workshops, such as Big Draw challenges, and other cut and paste sessions. For more fun from November to January, the courtyard is transformed into a magical ice-skating rink (with a Christmas tree, torch lights, and Christmas Arcade in season). While you slip around on the ice, imagine how the royal court jester might have entertained the future Queen Elizabeth I, who once lived here, or Anne of Denmark (married to James I) taking part in sumptuous masquerades with her ladies-in-waiting in the early 1600s.

KEEP IN MIND
Weekend and school holiday drop-in art or puppetry work shops for children run 11–4 and 2–4; check ahead for details or ask at the information desk at Seaman's Hall. There's Skate School and Penguin Club for kids in winter, although tickets (tel. 0844/847–1520) are popular, so book ahead; the website has info.

EATS FOR KIDS The **Courtauld Gallery Café** (020/784–2527) to the north of Fountain Court has a patio garden and funky teapots, and serves English cake, soups, and light meals. **Fernandez & Wells** (tel.020/7420–9408) has indoor and outdoor seats on the east side of the court, and serves up exceptional Spanish jamón sandwiches, eggs on sourdough, or Tuscan-cured meat platters for under £8.

SOUTH BANK

Taking you from Strauss to skateboarding, dance, music, poetry, plays, secondhand books and old movies, the South Bank arts zone and riverside promenade fizzes with high, medium, and low street culture and performance, in a remarkably captivating five-and-a-half mile stretch of the Thames Path between Westminster and Tower Bridges.

Starting at Westminster Bridge with its arresting views of the neo-Gothic Big Ben and Houses of Parliament, you'll find the former County Hall building, which now hosts reef sharks and stingrays at the London Aquarium, plus dodgems, arcades, and bowling lanes in the Namco Funscape. As you meander along, mind the crowds milling at the foot of the iconic London Eye wheel, and see if there's a giant carousel spinning round at Jubilee Gardens; either way, you'll no doubt have to dodge myriad living statues, break dancers, body poppers, or mime artists.

Next is the Royal Festival Hall, built for the Festival of Britain in 1951, and which has anchored the cultural blossoming of the adjacent Southbank Centre. Here you'll find family symphony concerts by the resident London Philharmonic Orchestra (look out

KEEP IN MIND

The Thames Path continues past the National Theatre to Blackfriars Bridge and the shops and restaurants of Gabriel's Wharf, and the Oxo Tower. Heading for London Bridge, you'll find the Tate Modern, Shakespeare's Globe, the Clink Prison Museum, *Golden Hinde*, Southwark Cathedral, and Borough Market.

MAKING THE MOST OF YOUR TIME
Serendipity is often the best way to approach the Southbank Centre. You might stumble across a wacky sound installation, find a Mariachi folk band from Mexico playing on a terrace, or happen upon the London Community Gospel Choir giving an open-air concert. The excellent Poetry Library hosts readings and storytelling for children, and the Purcell Room has appearances by famous kids' authors. The Royal Festival Hall's Spirit Level music learning space has technology for kids to experiment with composition, and look out for the food stalls at the weekly Real Food market (open Friday to Sunday, from 11 or noon, to 6–8 pm).

South Bank, Belvedere Rd., SE1.
Tube: Waterloo, Westminster

 Southbank Centre, 0844/875–0073;
www.southbankcentre.co.uk

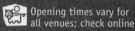 Opening times vary for
all venues; check online

  Daily

4 and up

for kid-friendly FUNharmonics weekend sessions), and the Philharmonia. The multitiered and marvelously batty and brutalist Southbank Centre fuses the RFH, the Queen Elizabeth Hall, the chamber-music-to-poetry-recital Purcell Room, the exemplary Haywood Gallery contemporary art gallery, and the Poetry Library.

Between them, they annually host some thousand paid performances of music, dance, and literature, up to six major art exhibitions, some 300 free foyer events and numerous workshops, many of which appeal specifically to kids—from the annual 50-event Imagine Children's Literature Festival to an inspiring concert by the Simón Bolivar Youth Orchestra of Venezuela or a session with a clown from Cirque-du-Soleil.

Next door under Waterloo Bridge is a daily open-air book market, the three awesome auditoriums of the National Theatre (#25), and the underrated BFI Southbank, which showcases 1,000 classic films a year on four screens, from Hitchcock to Kurosawa, and includes regular Film Fundays, with kids' workshops, storyboards, and Q&As with actors.

EATS FOR KIDS Enjoy English specialties at **Canteen** (tel. 0845/686–1122) at the Royal Festival Hall, where you'll find terrace tables, fish finger sandwiches, and blackberry and apple crumble, plus half-price kids' portions. Filling chicken tinga tacos (£3.95) or plaice burritos with green rice (£7.25) feature at the Mexican winner, **Wahaca** (tel. 020/7928–1876), below Queen Elizabeth Hall. Or tuck into £5.50 sausage or bacon sandwiches or kids' meals on Film Fundays at **Benugo Bar & Kitchen** (tel. 020/7401–9000) at BFI Southbank.

ST. PAUL'S CATHEDRAL

It may have the second-largest cathedral dome, and been inspired by St Peter's Basilica in Rome, but this was actually Sir Christopher Wren's *smaller* design to replace the cathedral destroyed in the Great Fire of 1666. St. Paul's took more than 35 years to build and still dominates London's skyline, having survived the Blitz of World War II. It has been the setting for momentous ceremonies, like the wedding of Charles and Diana or the Queen's Golden Jubilee service.

After you've tackled the sweeping front steps, plug into the free audio guide, which contains illuminating history, highlights, and quizzes. Then head for the quire (choir) and high altar, and crane your neck to see the bright mosaics of heavenly images. In contrast to Westminster Abbey, St. Paul's is spacious and relatively simple; Wren wanted to keep the clutter of memorials and monuments in the crypt. But do visit the American Memorial Chapel in the apse, dedicated to the 28,000 GIs who died during World War II while stationed in Britain or en route to the country.

EATS FOR KIDS In the crypt, the **Café at St Paul's** (020/7248–2469) offers a children's menu with fish fingers or cod and chips served with ice cream and a drink. Smart British-based choices for adults include Norfolk asparagus, wild mushroom tart, and Eaton Mess. Try kids' prawn cocktail, plaice-and-chips, fried chicken wings, or meatballs (£7.50) at Gordon Ramsay's Art Deco-style **Bread Street Kitchen** (tel. 020/7592–1616).

St. Paul's Churchyard, EC4.
Tube: Cannon St., St. Paul's

 020/7246-8348;
www.stpauls.co.uk

 £15 ages 17 and up, £6
children 6–17, £36 family

 Cathedral M–Sa 8:30–4;
galleries M–Sa 9:30–4:15

 5 and up

Climb the 259 steps to the Whispering Gallery to see the enormous dome, painted with sepia murals of St. Paul. You're now 99 feet above the floor, and you can whisper a message to someone on the other side, who may hear your echo. The interior dome is smaller than the exterior one and 60 feet lower; between the two a brick cone supports the 850-ton lantern, surmounted by a golden ball and cross. For the ultimate stair-climbing challenge—another 269, or 528 in total—and assuming you have a head for heights, climb the spiraling grated stairs to the open-air Golden Gallery, on top of the dome. The view of London and the shimmering Millennium Bridge is worth the hike.

Downstairs in the crypt are 200 memorials and grandiose tombs of heroes like the Duke of Wellington, Lord Nelson, Sir Winston Churchill, and Florence Nightingale, as well as the simple plaque for Wren himself, which reads: *"Reader, if you seek a monument, look around you."*

KEEP IN MIND

It's believed the first Saxon cathedral was built here by Mellitus (the first Bishop of London) in AD 604. A third cathedral burned down in 1087, and the Normans built another, which took 200 years. The fourth St. Paul's—Old St. Paul's—was decaying by the time of the 1666 Great Fire.

MAKING THE MOST OF YOUR TIME You'll need

firm shoes to scale the Whispering Gallery, and strong nerves to attempt the stairs to the balustrade outside the dome. (Older kids will love that final climb.) The one-hour Triforium Tour takes you to parts of the cathedral not open to the public with general admission, including the library, Wren's great model of the cathedral, and another bunch of stairs: the Geometric Staircase. This tour runs on Monday, Tuesday, and Friday and costs £19.50, including cathedral admission. The standard 10-plus group tour is a cheaper option at £3 adults, £1 children.

TATE BRITAIN

9

Just because the current buzz is all about Tate Modern (and justifiably so—*see* #8), don't miss Tate Britain. The greatest collection of British art anywhere, from 1500 to the present day, is showcased in bright, elegant, and suitably serene surroundings here at Millbank on the Thames. Exceptionally child-friendly, it's an absolute must, and after a visit you can jump on the Tate Boat and cruise 20 minutes downstream straight to Tate Modern on the Bankside and double-up on art for the day.

The 1897 Tate Britain gallery (the former Millbank Prison, which held convicts in Victorian times before they were transported to Australia as punishment) embraces everything from Old Masters and Pre-Raphaelites to contemporary artists and sculptors like Henry Moore, Lucian Freud, David Hockney, Sarah Lucas, Damien Hirst, and Chris Ofili.

The rooms are arranged chronologically and take you through a walk of 500 years of British art, however, kids are invariably drawn to a number of Victorian blockbusters, like John Everett Millais's haunting painting of the drowned Ophelia (1851) clutching

MAKING THE MOST OF YOUR TIME There are free drop-in Tiny Tate activity days for under-5s where kids might become part of an installation. Hands-on "Liminal" sculpture-focused sessions take place on weekends 11–3, and a venerable Art Trolley is wheeled out on weekends and school holidays 10–3.

KEEP IN MIND The two biggest geniuses of British landscape painting are generally considered to be John Constable and J.M.W. Turner. You can find the world's best collection of their works here, in the Clore Galleries. They both painted in the early 19th century, but what's even more surprising is that they both chose to focus many of their paintings on the same picturesque part of England—the counties of Norfolk and Suffolk, known collectively as East Anglia. Constable produced rural country scenes, while Turner favored the vibrant colors of sunsets, seascapes, and sail-powered battle ships.

Millbank, SW1.
Tube: Pimlico

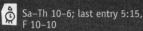
020/7887-8888;
www.tate.org.uk

Free

Sa–Th 10–6; last entry 5:15,
F 10–10

5 and up

wildflowers in a weeping brook, a tragic scene from Shakespeare's *Hamlet*. J.W. Waterhouse's *The Lady of Shalott* (1888) drips with Pre-Raphaelite romanticism and sentimentality, as it captures an Arthurian scene from Alfred, Lord Tennyson's poem of the same name.

A free app quiz trail will keep kids hunting and rooting through the 30-odd galleries, from historic Hogarths, Gainsboroughs, Blakes, Stubbs, and Whistlers, to J.M.W. Turner's swirling ship battle scenes and Francis Bacon's beastly and terrifying triptych, *Three Studies for Figures at the Base of a Crucifixion* (1944). Damien Hirst's pickled sheep in formaldehyde, *Away from the Flock* (1994), is a piece that will always hold kids' attention.

The gallery also encourages kids to sketch and scribble their way round. Head for the information desk and ask for an "A is For Britain" A-4 pack. These will get kids striking a pose in front of *Ophelia*, drawing famous British figures, and listing their top 10 Tate Britain paintings.

EATS FOR KIDS There are few cafés nearby, but hot and cold snacks including sandwiches, tartlets, and salads, can be found at the ground-floor **Café,** to the east of the lower Rotunda. The **Rex Whistler Restaurant** showcases a striking wall-length mural by Rex Whistler—*The Expedition in Pursuit of Rare Meats* (1927)—and is the more grown-up and expensive option—but no less friendly for that. It's famous for its fine wine list, but you can order reduced-price, smaller portions for kids from the main menu, which has a wide selection of fish and meat dishes.

TATE MODERN

As modern art galleries go, this one is a masterpiece of family-friendly programming and art. Poems, music, and artists' and kids' points of view—no art-speak here—prompt children to look at art in fun ways, determine their own opinions, and really engage. The building once housed Bankside Power Station, and in its modernist, high-tech conversion the *five-story* central Turbine Hall has kept its original industrial proportions—great for displaying oversize, wacky pieces of sculpture. Just walking in gives you the sense that anything can happen, and as you soon discover at this most-visited of modern-art museums, *it does*.

Along with trails of the seven-story behemoth, plus a "Tate Trumps" app to collect favorite exhibits, kids love the handheld multimedia guide (£4), which explores selected pieces with videos, quizzes, stills, and commentary—from Roy Lichtenstein's comic-like *Whaam!* painting to Dali's Surrealist dreamscape *Metamorphosis of Narcissus*. They also learn about techniques created by groundbreaking artists as they look at Henri Matisse's snail collage and Jackson Pollock's squiggles. Not only do kids find these pieces wild and

EATS FOR KIDS The **Tate Café** (Level 1, tel. 020/7887–8888) has floor-to-ceiling windows overlooking the Thames and St. Paul's Cathedral. Kids under 12 can eat free for lunch when an adult has a main, or alternatively the Brit-focused £5.20 kids' menu includes Cornish haddock fish fingers, cottage pie, and strawberry jelly. The views of St Paul's and Millennium Bridge are world-class spectacular at the **Restaurant at Tate Modern** (Level 6, tel. 020/8887–8888), where kids dine free for lunch (as above), or can enjoy mini pizza and banana split for £5.10.

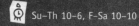

Bankside, SE1.
Tube: Blackfriars,
London Bridge, Southwark

 Free

 020/7887-8888;
www.tate.org.uk

Su–Th 10–6, F–Sa 10–10

 4 and up

attractive, they are encouraged to think about what the artist might (or might not) have been trying to achieve. Parents can join in the fun, too.

The Surrealist collection is always a winner with kids, from Man Ray's spiked *Cadeau*, to Calder's mobiles, and Giacometti's stick-like *Men and Women* sculptures. Joan Miró's quirky fantasia paintings and Magritte's playful conundrums go down well, and there are intriguing sculptures like Cornelia Parker's *Cold Dark Matter*, an exploded view of metal, wood, wire, plastic, and textiles, dangling in the air.

Be sure to venture down into the Tank—all raw-concrete and the world's first permanent dedicated performance art space—in three giant underground cylindrical former oil tanks that used to fire the old power station. Look for family-focused installations, off-base dance pieces, or avant-garde performances.

KEEP IN MIND
There are art books, films, games, and art timelines on the walls in the Interactive Zone (Level 4), plus Cubist objects to clamber on at the Under 5s Zone. Audio guides and sketch materials are available, and free daily gallery tours leave at 11, noon, 2, and 3. A dedicated Start team at the family concourse (Level 3) helps families on weekends and holidays.

MAKING THE MOST OF YOUR TIME Tate Modern commissions an artist each year to make a giant installation for the sloping Turbine Hall, and exhibits the invariably child-friendly installation from October to March. Rachel Whiteread filled the hall with 14,000 Artic-inspired translucent white, polyethylene boxes, and Colombian artist Doris Salcedo put a giant crack down the middle of the floor. Chinese artist Ai Weiwei poured 100 million tiny individually painted porcelain sunflower seeds into the Turbine Hall, although dust from the seeds proved to be a health hazard, and the public was barred from viewing it.

THAMES RIVER CRUISE

A leisurely cruise down the River Thames on a fine day from Westminster to Greenwich is quite simply one of the *best* ways to see London in its full, magnificent, *meandering*, gory, historic, glory.

Take the river route downstream that Henry VIII used to make to his beloved Tudor Greenwich Palace, although nowadays you'll be glad that this 4-mile journey only takes about 65 minutes. Jump on at the Westminster or London Eye Piers, and grab an open-air top-deck seat, and preferably sit at the side of the boat for the best panoramic views.

Leaving Big Ben, the Banqueting House, and Westminster Palace behind, your head will ping this way and that, like at a Wimbledon Final, as a corny gag-filled commentary by a Cockney ferryboatman highlights the key Thames-side landmarks and notorious curios on both banks of the river.

The River Thames has been at the heart of London life ever since the invading Roman general Julius Caesar referred to it to it by its Celtic name, Tamesis, in 54 BC.

KEEP IN MIND

"Frost Fairs" were held on the Thames during winters when the river has frozen solid. The first was in 1564 when stalls, sideshows, merry-go-rounds, and donkey races when set up on the ice near London Bridge. The last Frost Fair was in 1813.

MAKING THE MOST OF YOUR TIME City Cruises (tel. 020/740–0400) depart from Westminster, London Eye, and Tower Piers (next to the Tower of London) for Greenwich every 30 minutes daily (March–November) from 9:15 to 6:25. Round tickets are £15.50 for adults, £7.75 for under-16s, while £51 family tickets (2 adults, 3 kids) offer hop-on, hop-off travel. **Thames River Services** (tel. 020/7930–4097) leave from Westminster Pier for Greenwich every half an hour until 5 pm during peak season (April–October)—adults £13, kids £6.50, and family tickets £33 (2 adults, 3 kids). **Thames Clippers** commuter services have slightly cheaper tickets to Greenwich.

Westminster Pier, Victoria Embankment, SW1; London Eye Pier quay, South Bank, SE1. Tube: Westminster

 Check online

City Cruises, 020/7740-0400; Thames River Services, 020/7930-4097, www.citycruises.com or www.thamesriverservices.co.uk

City Cruises Mar–Nov, every 30 mins from 9:15, last boat from Greenwich 6:25 pm, Nov–Mar from 10, last boat Greenwich 4:50; TRS Apr–Oct every 30 mins, last boat from Greenwich 6, Oct–Apr every 40 mins from 10:20, last boat Greenwich 4:30

 4 and up

You'll pass the brutalist Southbank Centre, the luxury Savoy Hotel, and Cleopatra's Needle, a 1500 BC Egyptian obelisk presented to Britain in 1819, which contains a time capsule including a baby's bottle and a map of London.

You'll pass the old Royal palace Somerset House, the Oxo Tower, Millennium Bridge, Tate Modern, Waterloo Bridge (known as the Ladies' bridge, because it was built by women during WWII), Shakespeare's Globe, Southwark Cathedral, London Bridge (the old one was sold to an American in 1968), the Shard tower, HMS *Belfast*, the Tower of London and Traitors' Gate, and former working wharfs, like Hays Galleria (known as the Larder of London) and Butler's Wharf, next to the iconic Tower Bridge.

It's a mesmerizing river pageant, which continues past Execution dock (where pirates were hung, tarred, and gibbeted), the Mayflower pub (where the *Mayflower* set sail for Southampton and New England with the Pilgrim Fathers in 1621), the Isle of Dogs, and Canary Wharf, before stopping at the resplendent *Cutty Sark* tea-clipper at Greenwich Pier.

EATS FOR KIDS You can't go wrong with the kids' meals at **Giraffe** (tel. 020/7928–2004) at the Southbank Centre, six minutes from the London Eye Pier, where you'll find salmon with peas and sweet corn and a drink for £4.95. There are also beef hot dogs, sausage, Heinz baked beans and mash, and 99 sundaes for £4.25–£5.50. At Greenwich near the *Cutty Sark*, the artisan baker **Paul Rhodes** (tel. 020/8825–8995) does high-quality Parma ham baguettes, quiche Lorraine, and cheese and onion tarts for £4.80.

TOWER OF LONDON

"*S*end him to the Tower!*" was the royal command that filled many a quaking prisoner with dread, and those who entered by Traitors' Gate, on the Thames, were unlikely to return. Europe's best-preserved medieval castle, the Tower of London actually comprises 20 towers, added through the centuries. It's been a fortress, medieval palace, royal prison, mint, armory, and even the royal menagerie—with lions and polar bears. The original White Tower was built by William the Conqueror in 1078, who had it fortified to "overawe the Londoners." It still leaves visitors in awe 950 years later.

The 23,587-gem Crown Jewels are a relatively modern addition (from 1660), but their splendor is no less magnificent, as lines testify. Head to the Jewel House; once through the thick strong-room doors, you'll find 10 crowns bursting with jewels, scepters, golden orbs, swords, and sparkling rings, whose diamonds are the size of speckled eggs. The Queen wears the Imperial State Crown and Sceptre with the Cross—with the world's largest cut diamond, the 530-carat First Star of Africa—for the State Opening of Parliament.

EATS FOR KIDS The **New Armouries Café** serves fresh food, £4.50 kids' lunchboxes and traditional British fare from London markets, like fish from Billingsgate and roasts from Smithfield. The **Perkin Reveller** (tel. 020/3166–6949) on the Wharf just outside the Tower has £6.50 kids' menus, with breaded chicken strips or salmon and green beans, with ice cream. Outside the Tower, head under Tower Bridge for tony St Katherine's Dock, and try chicken strips or sausage and mash for £4.25 at the historic, wooden-beamed and atmospheric **The Dickens Inn** (tel. 020/748–2208).

Tower Hill, EC3.
Tube: Tower Hill

0844/482-7777 information,
0844/482-7799 tickets;
www.hrp.org.uk

Advance tickets £18 ages
16 and up, £9 children
5–15; gate prices £20.90
and £10.45; £47 family

Mar–Oct, Tu–Sa 9–5.30, Su–M 10–5.30;
Nov–Feb, Tu–Sa 9–4.30, Su–M 10–4.30;
last entry 30 mins before closing

4 and up

To find out how they were made, visit the Martin Tower's Crowns and Diamonds exhibit.

Aristocratic traitors were imprisoned in the Beauchamp Tower, where they killed time chiseling graffiti in the walls. Only nobles were beheaded here, and they're listed behind the executioner's block on Tower Green. The ghost of Anne Boleyn, Henry VIII's second wife, is said to haunt the chapel of St. Peter ad Vincula and has been seen walking around the White Tower with her head under her arm. To get an idea of what life was like, go to the Wakefield Tower, where costumed guides answer questions and tell tales of those sometimes terrible times. Weapons fanatics should shoot for the elaborate displays of flintlock pistols and swords in the White Tower. Check out Henry VIII's extra-extra-large armor and mini versions for little princes, and the old arsenal, where gunpowder barrels line the walls. Look out for the six ravens—legend says that if they ever leave the Tower, the kingdom will fall.

KEEP IN MIND
With stories of executions, child-slaying, and medieval torture, the Tower has ghost stories and legends galore. The ghosts of the young princes in the Tower, Edward and Richard, who disappeared here in 1483, are said to appear holding hands in their nightgowns before fading into the walls of the Bloody Tower.

MAKING THE MOST OF YOUR TIME
To avoid lining up for tickets, buy tickets from any Underground station or purchase by phone or online. Annual family tickets cost £83 and allow two adults and up to six children entry to five royal palaces, including Hampton Court and Kensington Palace. At the Tower entrance, check the schedule of daily events and ask for guided Yeoman Warder tours. These centuries-old guards (also called "Beefeaters") wearing red-and-gold uniforms lead free tours every half hour daily from near the main entrance (last tour 3:30 in summer, 2:30 in winter).

TRAFALGAR SQUARE

5

No kid's first trip to London is complete without clambering up onto the backs or paws of one of the four bronze lions guarding the base of Nelson's Column at Trafalgar Square, the city's famous main public square, and sometime piazza, tourist attraction, milling around spot, and periodic *place politique*. Mounting the surprisingly slippery lions takes a bit of work, but once up, kids are rewarded with 360-degree views, which take in the grand porticoed entrance to the National Gallery, the handsome National Portrait Gallery, the great spire of James Gibbs' 1726 St Martin-in-the-Fields church, Canada and South Africa Houses, and the ceremonial triple-arched Admiralty Arch, which leads straight down the Mall to Buckingham Palace.

Beside Sir Edwin Lutyins fountains (erected to reduce space, and by default, *riotous assembly*) is the 170-foot Nelson's Column, a giant Corinthian granite column and statue of Admiral Lord Nelson, a great Royal Naval commander who was shot and killed defeating Napoleon and the Spanish Navy at the Battle of Trafalgar in 1805.

EATS FOR KIDS

Sit at outdoor benches at the **Café in the Square** (tel. 020/7983–4882) at the bottom of the central staircase in Trafalgar Square, where you'll find sandwiches, and light bites like jacket potatoes. Also see National Gallery (#28), National Portrait Gallery (#26), and London Brass Rubbing Centre (#39).

KEEP IN MIND Moored on a traffic island to the south of Trafalgar Square is a bronze equestrian statue of Charles I staring down Whitehall to the scene of his execution. The statue marks the place where eight of the signatories to Charles I's death warrant were disemboweled in 1660. It's also the spot of the original Charring Cross that stood here until 1647—stone crosses erected by Edward I to mark the resting places of the funeral cortège of this beloved first wife Eleanor of Castile, when her body was brought back from Nottingham to Westminster Abbey in 1291.

Trafalgar Square, WC2.
Tube: Charing Cross

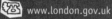 www.london.gov.uk

 Free

Daily

All ages

Trafalgar Square was built by John Nash in 1844 but it sits on what used to be known as the King's Mews, which was the home of the royal falcons during the reign of Edward I in the 12th century and later home to royal stables under Henry VIII and Elizabeth I. During the English Civil War in the 1640s it was turned into a barracks for the Parliamentary Army, and converted into a prison for 4,500 captured Royalists in 1645.

Today, look out for the Fourth Plinth—originally intended to hold an equestrian statue— in the northwest corner of the square. It is now used to display temporary public artwork. Hunt down the world's smallest police station—big enough for one policeman and a hotline to Scotland Yard—located inside a lamppost. It was used as a lookout to keep an eye on demonstrations and riots, but it's now a storage cupboard for cleaners. Can you find it?

MAKING THE MOST OF YOUR TIME Besides
political rallies and gatherings (like the Poll Tax riots of 1990, or Stop the War march against the invasion of Iraq in 2003), Trafalgar Square celebrates national sporting triumphs (2012 Olympics and Team Great Britain), and hosts cultural events, like celebrating Chinese New Year, St. Patrick's Day, or New Year's Eve. Look for carol singing, and the Christmas ceremony where the Norwegian city of Oslo presents London with a Christmas tree, a 50-year-old Norwegian spruce, as gratitude for support during WWII.

WARNER BROS. STUDIO TOUR:
THE MAKING OF HARRY POTTER

4

Yell *"Expelliarmus!!"* to Death Eaters, drink Butterbeer, or jump aboard a broomstick and the Knight Bus or sit in Weasley's blue Ford Anglia, at the magical Warner Bros. Studio Tour: The Making of Harry Potter, at Leavesden studio near Watford, where all eight Harry Potter films were made—the most successful film series ever.

The behind-the-scenes studio, set, costume, props, and special effects tour wows Harry Potter fans—and nonfans—alike because of the fantastically detailed sets and scenes at the 150,000-square-foot studio, and the passionate staff on hand to guide you through the world of Harry, Hermione, Ron, and the Hogwarts School of Witchcraft and Wizardry.

Your timed tour kicks off with a cinema screening on the making of *Harry Potter*, which then lifts up to reveal the set of the famous ancient wooden beamed and candlelit Great Hall at Hogwarts—scene of the classic Start-of-Term and Halloween Feasts, the Dueling Club, Yule Ball, and Apparition lessons.

KEEP IN MIND If you can't make Leavesden studio, you can spot lots of locations in London where scenes from *Harry Potter* were filmed. Harry flies along the River Thames on his broomstick, for example, past the London Eye and Tower Bridge in *Harry Potter and the Order of the Phoenix*, and Platform 9¾ from where the steam train departs to Hogwarts is really Platform 4 at King's Cross station; look for the plaque and half a shopping trolley disappearing into the wall. The Reptile House in London Zoo is where Harry first speaks the serpent language Parseltongue in *Harry Potter and the Philosopher's Stone*.

Aerodrome Way, Leavesden, Hertfordshire, WD25. Rail: Watford Junction

08450/840-900;
www.wbstudiotour.co.uk

 £29 age 16 and over, £21.50 ages 5–15, under 4 free; £85 family (2 adults, 2 children)

 Daily from 10; last tour 4–6:30

4 and up

After the screening and set visit, you're free to explore the atmospheric and incredibly detailed Dumbledore's Office, Gryffindor's Common Room, Hagrid's Hut, a Potions class, and Professor Umbridge's Office at the Ministry of Magic. You can explore animatronics and meet infamous beasts—Buckbeak and the giant eagle Hippogriff, Fawkes the Phoenix, and Basilisk, King of the Serpents. There's also the blind Acromantula Aragog, and the house-elf Kreacher, who served at the House of Black.

Ring a doorbell and visit the Dursley family, then wander down the set of Diagon Alley, where you can peer into Ollivanders Wand Shop ("Makers of fine wands since 382 BC"), Flourish and Blotts bookshop, Eeylps Owl Emporium, and Gringotts Wizarding Bank (operated by goblins). The impressive model of Hogwarts Castle built for *Harry Potter and the Philospher's Stone* is an awe-inspiring sight and star exhibit, twinkling with 2,500 fiber-optic lanterns and torches, and giving the impression of shadows passing through the hallways. Give yourselves at least three to four hours to fully Muggle up on this studio tour.

MAKING THE MOST OF YOUR TIME
Book timed tickets in advance, and travel 30 minutes from London Euston to Watford Junction railway station, where there are shuttle buses (run by Mullany's Coaches) that run to the studio tour at Leavesden studio every 30 minutes (journey time, 15 minutes). Plan to arrive 20 minutes before your allotted entry ticket time. There are free Activity Passports with trails, plus apps and souvenir guides available, although the tour is so engrossing that bells and whistles are hardly necessary.

EATS FOR KIDS
The **Studio Cafe** in the foyer has soups, sandwiches, and salads, plus cakes and buns. Or you stop halfway round the tour at **The Backlot for Butterbeer** (a small tankard is £2.95), and you can sit and enjoy your own sandwiches and picnic.

WEST END SHOW

With some of the world's greatest stages and most historic theaters (the earliest dates from 1683, at Sadlers Wells), London offers the best theater and musicals in the world, and a trip to a dazzling West End show—replete with greasepaint, buzz, footlights, plush velvet seats, and gilt-edged theaters—is a truly magical treat for kids ages seven and up.

With about 50 theaters crammed into the West End—mainly dotted around Shaftesbury Avenue, Covent Garden, the Haymarket, and the Strand—spectacular new productions pop up every few months or so vying to be the new, best, shiniest, *biggest-ever*, smash hit. If a show bombs, and is panned by the critics, however, it can close within weeks, or even days.

For a rain check on what's on offer, it's worth visiting Visit London (visitlondon.com), the Official London Theatre site (officiallondontheatre.co.uk), or london-theatreland.co.uk, which also highlight the popular long-standing kids' favorites, that continue

KEEP IN MIND

At the Les Miz Kids Club workshops on Saturday you can go back stage for behind-the-scenes tours, including drama workshops, packed-lunch, a meeting with a cast member, and certificate of attendance. Look for kids' Christmas pantomimes (or "pantos"), a holiday tradition for locals, November–February.

MAKING THE MOST OF YOUR TIME

Buy tickets in advance from theater box offices by phone or online, or line up in person at the theater for a limited number of tickets for same-day performances, or for late returns. In the second half of August, kids' tickets are free for West End shows during **Kids Week** (tel. 020/7557–6799), when an adult buys a full-price ticket. You can also line up at the official **TKTS** ticket booth in the Clocktower building in Leicester Square (Monday–Sunday 9–7, Sunday 10:30–4.30) for discounted or same-day West End show tickets.

West End, Tube: Covent Garden,
Piccadilly Circus, Leicester Square

www.visitlondon.com;
www.officiallondontheatre.co.uk;
www.london-theatreland.co.uk

Check theaters online

Check times online

7 and up

to run and run. Les Misérables has been going strong for 20 years, and is a moving—even tear-jerking—musical adaptation of Victor Hugo's 19th-century epic among the wretched *san-culottes* of Paris that leads up to the June Rebellion in 1832. Other faves like *Billy Elliot, Shrek The Musical, The Lion King, Mamma Mia!, Oliver!, Matilda, Grease,* and *The Phantom of the Opera* are all-singin', all-dancin' five-star productions that will get your kids swaying and singing in the aisles, or at least tapping along, and inspired. The genius puppet-show *War Horse*—a tale of a boy, Albert, and his horse, Joey, who's sold to the cavalry during WWI—is the National Theatre's most successful play ever, and now shows at the New London Theatre in Drury Lane. Roald Dahl's *Charlie and the Chocolate Factory* wows on the same street at the Theatre Royal.

The Royal Opera House, Sadler's Wells Theatre, and the English National Opera all have fabulous shortened operas, ballets, or dance performances aimed specifically at kids—from *Jane Eyre* to *The Nutcracker*.

EATS FOR KIDS Enjoy £8.50 kids' meals (Monday–Sunday, noon–6:30) in mini opera boxes with live opera music and clapping (Sunday lunchtime, plus Sunday and Monday evening) by pros from the Royal Opera House at the theater-themed and West End showstopper **Sarastro** (tel. 020/ 78360–0101) on Drury Lane, named for a character from Mozart's *Magic Flute*. Or chose £6.95 kids' meals like chicken breast, steak pie, or fishcakes amid colonial-style palm trees at theater-land stand-by, **Browns**, (tel. 020/ 749–5050) on St. Martin's Lane.

WESTMINSTER ABBEY

A beautiful early English Gothic masterpiece with flying buttresses, sweeping arches, and a 102-foot soaring nave, Westminster Abbey—founded by St. Dunstan in AD 960—has hosted coronations since William the Conqueror's in 1066 and overflows with royal tombs, monuments, and memorials to national heroes. From the Cosmati onyx, glass, and stone floor to fabulously decorated fan-vault ceiling, there's much to admire.

Worn effigies of medieval monarchs, and missing mosaic stones stolen over the centuries encircle the ancient St Edward's Chapel—where St Edward the Confessor is enshrined. Beneath the steps to the Henry VII Chapel, the solemn oak Coronation Chair used by 38 kings and queens since 1308 bears the graffiti of naughty Westminster schoolboys. Inside the Henry VII Chapel, which is dominated by the tombs of King Henry and his queen (Elizabeth); Elizabeth I, her half-sister Mary I (beneath her), and cousin Mary, Queen of Scots are entombed as well. A marble urn holds the remains of the young princes, Edward I and Richard, Duke of York, presumed murdered in the Tower of London. Poets'

EATS FOR KIDS The **Wesley Café** (tel. 020/7222–8010) is a popular budget haunt opposite the Abbey, in Methodist Central Hall, Storey's Gate. You can grab a hot or cold meal for around £7, including salads, sandwiches, and panini. Or head down to 53 Whitehall toward Trafalgar Square for **The Clarence** (tel. 020/7930–4808) wood-beamed gastro-pub and £5 kids' hamburger or fish-and-chips half-price meals.

Broad Sanctuary, SW1.
Tube: Westminster

Abbey and museum
£16 adults, £6 children
11–18, under 11 free

Abbey M, T, Th, and F 9:30–4:30 (W until 7), Sa
9–2:30, closed for some services, Su worship only;
museum daily 10:30–4; College Garden T–Th 10–4

020/7222–5152;
www.westminster-abbey.org

6 and up

Corner is full of memorials to literary giants including Chaucer, Hardy, Dickens, and Shakespeare. Scientists Newton and Darwin are in the nave, near Ben Jonson (buried standing up, because he couldn't afford a coffin). The Tomb of the Unknown Warrior commemorates all who have lost their lives in war.

The Westminster Abbey Museum brings tomb residents to life through wax effigies: Henry VII's was taken from his death mask; Charles II's is richly adorned; and Elizabeth I's is displayed in a corset. Search for the ring she gave her favorite, the Earl of Essex, along with its romantic story. The octagonal Chapter House (where a chapter from the Scriptures was read daily) has eight shafts carrying the vaulted ceiling, with wooden seats encircling the original tiled floor. The 13th-century Cloisters were used by monks for meditation and exercise. Note the spires, buttresses, and gargoyles across the enclosed cloister garden. Reflect on the rich history of this ancient place in the College Garden, which was tended by Benedictine monks for more than 1,000 years.

KEEP IN MIND

Photography is not allowed within the Abbey, but pictures can be found in the stunning color guidebooks and postcards on sale at the Abbey Bookshop, outside the west entrance, and in the Westminster Abbey Museum. These show many of the sacred and ancient places not often open to visitors, such as the Jericho Parlour and Jerusalem Chamber.

MAKING THE MOST OF YOUR TIME

Families can book a 90-minute verger-led tour (£3 per person) that starts at the North Door and takes in the Shrine (including the tomb of Saint Edward the Confessor), the Royal tombs, Poet's Corner, the Cloister, and the Nave. Alternatively, pick up a Children's Trail and a free one-hour handheld audio guide from the information desk near the North Door.

WINDSOR CASTLE

I n the 1070s, William the Conqueror chose a great place for his fortress, close to the Thames, Windsor forest, and London. Though the multiturreted stone castle has grown much over the centuries (to 1,000 rooms), it remains the world's oldest occupied castle. Today it still dominates the landscape, towering above the pretty town of old Windsor and neighboring Eton, across the Thames, and it can clearly be seen from the motorway heading west from London. Whether viewed from inside or out, Windsor Castle is a sight to behold, especially for princess-, knight-, and wizard-loving kids.

The fabulously ornate State Apartments contain Old Master paintings (Rubens, Rembrandt, and Canaletto), gilt, chintz, china, and chandeliers galore, but the Grand Staircase and Vestibule's old weaponry—shiny swords, muskets, and rifles in cases, and crisscrossed weapons hung on high walls—will probably entice kids far more. You can see Henry VIII's armor of massive girth and the bullet that killed Lord Nelson at the Battle of Trafalgar. One of the oldest rooms, St. George's Hall, was beautifully restored after a fire in

KEEP IN MIND

Be sure to call ahead to confirm opening times and to make sure the State Apartments are not closed for a royal banquet.

MAKING THE MOST OF YOUR TIME

There are free two-hour audio tours (with kids' versions, ages 7–11), activity trails, and free frequent 30-minute Castle Precinct tours, plus art activities in the Moat room on the first Saturday of the month. You can also spend a lovely afternoon at Eton Brocas, the pretty meadows sloping down to the river, where you can watch boats, royal swans, and ducks go by.

Castle Hill, Berkshire. Rail: Windsor and Eton Central or Windsor and Eton Riverside

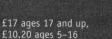 £17 ages 17 and up, £10.20 ages 5–16

020/7766–7304; www.royalcollection.org.uk

Mar–Oct, daily 9:45–5:15 (last entry 4); Nov–Feb, daily 9:45–4:15 (last entry 3)

 All ages

1992. It's lined with suits of knightly armor bearing lances pointing to the ceiling, which is emblazoned with the coats of arms of all the Knights of the Garter. At one end, the royal champion knight is poised, gauntlet raised, ready to throw down a challenge; this wasn't a usual occurrence but rather a coronation ritual.

The most charming item is Queen Mary's Doll House (Queen Elizabeth's grandmother), made by Sir Edwin Lutyens and 1,500 artists. With a 2,518-piece silver dinner set, everything in the mansion was a faithful copy of 1924 furnishings, all of which work, from the electric lights to the gramophone. The cellar contains miniature bottles of rare wine, as well as reproductions of its books and paintings. What little girl could resist playing with these mini treasures? It's positively enchanting, as are the larger dolls' trousseaux belonging to the young princesses Elizabeth and Margaret; designed by Dior and other great couturiers of the 1930s, they are displayed in the adjoining room. The centuries-old tradition of Changing the Guard (#63) takes place on alternate days; check ahead for schedules.

EATS FOR KIDS There is nothing to eat within the castle, but old Windsor has plenty of choices. The **Riverside Restaurant** (10 Thames Side, tel. 01753/620–010) has a prime spot on the Thames; find English classics for kids, like sausage and mash, fish strips, and chicken salad for £6.95, as well as outdoor seating. The friendly, 1645 old-world **Drury House Restaurant** (4 Church St., tel. 01753/863–734) has wood paneling, fireplaces, English roasts, homemade pies, and traditional afternoon teas. Try hot English gammon white baguette sandwiches with chips for £5.95.

CLASSIC GAMES

"I SEE SOMETHING YOU DON'T SEE AND IT IS BLUE." Stuck for a way to get your youngsters to settle down in a museum? Sit them on a bench in the middle of a room and play this vintage favorite. The leader gives just one clue—the color—and everybody guesses away.

"I'M GOING TO THE GROCERY STORE..." The first player begins, "I'm going to the grocery store and I'm going to buy...," finishing the sentence with the name of an object, found in grocery stores, that begins with the letter "A." The second player repeats what the first player has said, and adds the name of another item that starts with "B." The third player repeats everything that has been said so far and adds something that begins with "C," and so on through the alphabet. Anyone who skips or misremembers an item is out (or decide up front that you'll give hints to all who need 'em). You can modify the theme depending on where you're going that day, as "I'm going to X and I'm going to see..."

FAMILY ARK Noah had his ark—here's your chance to build your own. It's easy: Just start naming animals and work your way through the alphabet, from antelope to zebra.

PLAY WHILE YOU WAIT

NOT THE GOOFY GAME Have one child name a category. (Some ideas: first names, last names, animals, countries, friends, feelings, foods, hot or cold items, clothing.) Then take turns naming things that fall into it. You're out if you name something that doesn't belong in the category—or if you can't think of another item to add. When only one person remains, start again. Choose categories depending on where you're going or where you've been—historic topics if you've seen a historic sight, animal topics before or after the zoo, upside-down things if you've been to the circus, and so on. Make the game harder by choosing category items in A-B-C order.

DRUTHERS How do your kids really feel about things? Just ask. "Would you rather eat worms or hamburgers? Hamburgers or candy?" Choose serious and silly topics—and have fun!

BUILD A STORY "Once upon a time there lived . . ." Finish the sentence and ask the rest of your family, one at a time, to add another sentence or two. If you can, record the narrative so you can enjoy your creation again and again.